Praise for *Feminist Freedom Warriors*

"There are some books that w[...] use they are drawn from the experi[...] n-uine difference. This is one of t[...] [...]ns from, and conversations betwee[...] [...]m warriors, this book is a reminder of just how mu[..]h we need revolutionary, decolonial, anticapitalist, and antiracist feminism; how in fighting against structures, we are fighting for our lives. Each of these accounts of becoming and being feminists committed to radical transformation teaches us just how much we can do from what has been done; how we can make use of our imaginations, words, memories, knowledge, feelings, connections, and alliances in the project of building a more just world. This is a deeply inspiring and inspired collection."

—Sara Ahmed, author of *Living a Feminist Life*

"In *Feminist Freedom Warriors* liberation is historicized, imagined, and enacted as contested struggle and dialogue. The intellectual-activist thinkers within explain that feminist praxis—poetics, pedagogies, and activism—is an ongoing refusal of global capitalism and colonialism. Comprising stories and interviews, *Feminist Freedom Warriors* shows that engendering political change, across racial and sexual identifications, is tied to the uneasy work of imagining solidarities outside our present (neoliberal) system of knowledge. What stands out, beautifully and urgently, is the praxis of sharing how to refuse infrastructures of violence. *Feminist Freedom Warriors* captures how sharing and talking and learning, and the struggle to collaborate, are tied to the grounded work of building new futures."

—Katherine McKittrick, associate professor, Department of Gender Studies, Queen's University

"This collection brings together feminist visionaries to think deeply about how we sustain our movements, each other, and ourselves in and through ongoing feminist struggle. Mohanty's and Carty's dialogues with the contributors reveal crucial insights into building and theorizing multi-issue movements that rely on intersectional, antiracist, transnational feminisms. The collaborative endeavor illuminates the persistent intellectual capaciousness and radical hope of these scholar-activists. The contributors' complex engagements with feminist theory and praxis across geopolitical frameworks reaffirm coalitional possibilities so necessary in these turbulent times."

—T. Jackie Cuevas, author of *Post-Borderlandia*

Feminist Freedom Warriors

Genealogies, Justice, Politics, and Hope

Chandra Talpade Mohanty
and Linda E. Carty

with generous assistance from Taveeshi Singh

Haymarket Books
Chicago, Illinois

Published in 2018 by
Haymarket Books
P.O. Box 180165
Chicago, IL 60618
773-583-7884
www.haymarketbooks.org
info@haymarketbooks.org

ISBN: 978-1-60846-897-3

Distributed to the trade in the US through Consortium Book Sales
and Distribution (www.cbsd.com) and internationally through
Ingram Publisher Services International (www.ingramcontent.com).

This book was published with the generous support of Lannan
Foundation and Wallace Action Fund.

Special discounts are available for bulk purchases by organizations
and institutions. Please call 773-583-7884 or email
info@haymarketbooks.org for more information.

Cover artwork from "Migration Is Beautiful" by Favianna Rodriguez.

Printed in the United States.

Entered into digital printing August 2020.

Library of Congress Cataloging-in-Publication data is available.

10 9 8 7 6 5 4 3 2

Contents

Acknowledgments

We are deeply grateful to the participants to date in the ongoing Feminist Freedom Warriors video archive project (feministfreedomwarriors .org).

Profound gratitude to all of our collaborators and assistants on this project—Taveeshi Singh, whose dedication, creativity, and smarts are integral to both the website and this book, and Kim E. Powell, Marlon Walcott, Jingyi Wang, and Breanna Dickson for impeccable artistic and technical support.

Introduction

An Archive of Feminist Activism

Conversations with Margo Okazawa-Rey,
Angela Y. Davis, Himani Bannerji,
Minnie Bruce Pratt, Amina Mama, Aída
Hernández-Castillo, and Zillah Eisenstein

Linda E. Carty and Chandra Talpade Mohanty

> *The value of feminism or the value of antiracist, anticapitalist,*
> *anti-imperialist feminisms that are Marxist-inflected feminisms*
> *is that it allows us to think about the framework of our analysis*
> *or of our organizing at the same time as we use that framework to*
> *think about whatever it is we are examining. That is a habit that*

most people have not been able to embrace, because it is a habit that contravenes disciplinary thinking—in disciplinary thinking the framework is what enables everything else, so once you begin challenging the framework, everything falls apart. And feminism allows us to trouble the framework, allow things to fall apart, and at the same time put them back together. It allows us to imagine something entirely different.

—Angela Y. Davis

Feminism is at stake in how we generate knowledge; in how we write, who we cite. I think of feminism as a building project: if our texts are worlds, they need to be made out of feminist materials. Feminist theory is world-making. This is why we need to resist positioning feminist theory as simply or only a tool, in the sense of something that can be used in theory, only then to be put down or put away. It should not be possible to do feminist theory without being a feminist, which requires an active ongoing commitment to live one's life in a feminist way.

—Sara Ahmed, *Living a Feminist Life*

This book is a labor of love and sisterhood. It grows out of and is anchored in an ongoing digital archive project called Feminist Freedom Warriors (FFW), begun in 2015 (feministfreedomwarriors.org). The digital archive project was born out of our engagement with anticapitalist, antiracist feminist struggles as women of color from the Global South. FFW is a project about cross-generational histories of feminist activism addressing economic, antiracist, social justice, and anticapitalist issues across national borders. These are stories of sister-comrades, many of whom we have worked and struggled with over the years, whose ideas, words, actions, and visions of economic and social justice continue to inspire us to stay the course. The book is a companion to the larger digital project, highlighting the stories and analytical frameworks of seven prominent feminist scholar activists: Margo Okazawa-Rey, Angela Y. Davis, Himani Bannerji, Minnie Bruce Pratt, Amina Mama, Aída Hernández-Castillo, and Zillah Eisenstein.

Our conversations with these sister-comrades tell stories of politicization, of coming to consciousness and developing revolutionary, anticapitalist feminist commitments. We believe these narratives are necessary at this historical moment, as they help sustain radical struggles against neoliberal, transnational capital, carceral, national-security-driven nation-states, and the rise of racist, right-wing, authoritarian regimes in the United States and around the world. The seven scholar-activists featured here speak about their different and similar place-based genealogies of political engagements in anticapitalist, antiracist, anti-imperialist, LGBTQ, women's liberation, and indigenous feminist movements in the United States, Canada, Mexico/Latin America, India, and the Asian and African diasporas. Individually, and collectively, these scholar-activists illustrate the deep and significant connections between the personal and the political by (1) mapping their histories of coming of age within deeply oppressive, racist, colonialist, and hetero-patriarchal geopolitical contexts and (2) describing their journeys within social justice movements that anchor their analytic and theoretical frameworks and vision for economic justice. The stories are testament to Amina Mama's claim in chapter 5 that people are transformed within movements: "Our movements have inequalities within them, because we are formed in conventional, classed societies. Within movements we have to change ourselves as well as achieve things for women."

All seven women have been or are connected to the academy in their various landscapes—Angela, Margo, Zillah, and Minnie Bruce in the United States; Himani in Canada and India; Amina in Nigeria, the UK, South Africa, and now the United States; and Aída in Mexico. All of them have been involved in multiple social justice movements, sometimes in key leadership roles, and all have produced knowledge that has had an impact on a broad range of intellectual and political projects. Archiving these stories, then, is a political project about challenging mainstream narratives of feminism, of communism and "the left," and mapping the complexity of identity-based social movements, and of intellectual and political work in the academy. Often, mainstream narratives separate intellectual work from activist or movement work. Sometimes these are narratives where the production of knowledge, or intellectual production, is seen as institutionalized and abstracted from what is happening on the ground. However, much of our own work, and that of our sister-comrades, has been about figuring out those connections and being completely convinced that because communities struggle on the basis of ideas and visions of justice and equity, the intellectual and political work of knowledge production is always key to all forms of social movements and resistance. Thus, we talk about the individual place-based stories and narratives of coming of age as politicized feminists in different communities and parts of the world, but we also highlight what these reflections say about the movements on the ground and the geopolitical, ideological, as well as intellectual and political context in which these anticapitalist frameworks were generated. We draw attention to how particular kinds of connections across borders are made, and we suggest how this kind of thinking and activism leads to an expansive imagination of what radical transformation needs to be.

So for the sisters who have contributed to this book, their experiences pushed them into activism, and those experiences came out of particular locations, their own genealogies, and their commitment to be part of a liberation movement. So much of this is organic for them, but then there is a kind of unspoken, unmapped solidarity that we can now recognize existed. Thus, for instance, at the time when Angela and Margo are engaged in developing some of the key theoretical frameworks of Black anticapitalist feminist politics, Himani is engaged in a critique of the deeply patriarchal frames of postcolonial communist cultures in Bengal, and the racialized parameters of feminist movements in Canada. Similarly, Amina develops her feminist critique of the patriarchal, militarized postcolonial African state in the context of left, anticolonial, anticapitalist movements in Nigeria and the UK, and Aída comes to understand the misogynist politics and culture of the Mexican left and goes on to anchor her own scholarship and activism in collaborations with indigenous women in Latin America. In addition, like Angela, Zillah comes of age as a white woman in a communist, antiracist household engaged in the civil rights movement in the

United States, while Minnie Bruce struggles with a deeply racist landscape in the US South, developing a radical antiracist feminist politics within the context of the women's liberation and gay liberation movements in the 1960s and '70s. In each of these cases, our sister-comrades develop theoretical frameworks and activist commitments that are clearly connected to larger social movements on the horizon—in each case these frameworks arise from particular sociopolitical and cultural contexts but are not bound by these contexts. These genealogies are important—not because they are comprehensive, not because they are universal, not even because these are extraordinary women, but because as scholar-activists they emerge out of certain historical moments in particular geopolitical sites, and they reflect, theorize, analyze, and engage in movements that are concretely based in those historical landscapes but illustrate that forms of connections, crossing borders, and solidarities are possible.

After all, this is how Margo, Angela, Himani, Minnie Bruce, Amina, Aída, and Zillah live their lives. And this is what Taveeshi, our youngest sister scholar-activist, having worked closely with us on this project, picks up on in her "Postscript" on the politics of refusal and hope. So this volume is as much about living a politically conscious life as theorizing what happens in movements, or being an activist, or being a scholar, or being both—and feminism is a key ingredient. As Zillah Eisenstein (chapter 8) says, "My hope is for a deeply revolutionary antiracist feminism that embraces the complexity of the new meanings of racism and the new meanings of a misogyny that are no longer homogeneous categories. . . . Given the different layers of class, and therefore of different experiences of gender and race, it seems to me if we do not come to that complexity, we cannot have a feminism that matters, and for me feminism is the heart of any possibility."

The Urgency of a Decolonial, Anticapitalist, Antiracist Resistance

This is a time when the multiple communities we hold dear are engaged in some of the most urgent struggles of our times. In the United

States, Europe, India, Africa, and Latin America, there are struggles against fascism, Islamophobia, and corporate greed; struggles against racism, police brutality, immigrant and migrant rights, and deportation. In the United States, we see struggles against the proposed "Muslim ban" and its impact on academic communities; struggles for health care and reproductive rights; struggles for economic justice; prison abolition struggles; the Movement for Black Lives and its multiple incarnations across the United States and Europe; struggles for disability rights; struggles for indigenous land rights and sovereignty; the January 2017 Women's March, which was the largest mass mobilization of women in the United States, with sister marches around the world (followed by the similar January 2018 women's marches); the women's strike on International Women's Day (March 8, 2017) calling for a feminism for the 99 percent; an antiracist, anticapitalist, anti-imperialist feminism that takes on the proto-fascist shift of our political landscapes now; and so on. In the academy, of course, we face the increasing corporatization and militarization of university practices and the commodification and privatization of social justice claims. At the time of this writing, Donald Trump has been in office for a year, and since his inauguration we have witnessed hundreds of protests and rallies focused on a range of issues from education, immigration, water and land justice, reproductive and land rights, workers' rights, and others in multiple cities and towns across the United States and around the world.

Many of these struggles have feminist and women organizers at the forefront. Feminism matters—a feminism that is anchored in decolonizing, antiracist, anticapitalist, transnational commitments keeps us alive and gives us hope. And that is what this volume illustrates: that it is the creation of alliances and solidarities across gender, race, class, sexual, and national divides that point the way forward. After all, it is often the case that subaltern and decolonizing feminisms in different national contexts have more in common with one another than with mainstream feminisms in their own contexts. The stories of the feminist scholar-activists in these pages provide us with analytic tools, strategies, and modes of organizing and building transnational communities of struggle that we desperately need in these times when there are claims to so-called alternative facts, and when all forms of racial, religious, gender, and class discrimination are normalized by authoritarian regimes in countries around the world.

Building social movements in this era of neoliberal capitalism requires coalition building across differences that many of the participants in this volume speak about. This is an urgent moment in which neoliberal structures and practices have been particularly virulent against the work of anticapitalist, antiracist feminists. All of the sister-comrades here share a common understanding of how the governance practices of the neoliberal capitalist state have negatively impacted and continue to impact their own lives and work and that of their individual and collective communities and thus why resistance is urgent and necessary.

As scholar-activists they are acutely aware that whether they are in the richer Global North, where most are currently located, or in the comparatively poorer Global South, they are engaged in necessary anticapitalist, antiracist feminist struggle that is circumscribed by the ruling relations of the US state and its global economic hegemony and sphere of influence. This is manifested as oppressive (sometimes violent) state practice whether in the North or the South. These "national security" corporatized states confront us through hostile relations and actions that threaten to erase all the gains that emancipatory social movements have made over the last forty-plus years.

Forms of neoliberal governance structures have devastated the lives of the most marginalized peoples in both the North and the South, and it is not accidental that most of their victims are poor people and people of color, the populations that all of the sister-comrades here are committed to or work with directly. This is what is central in all of the narratives in this book: working against states that have no moral or ethical compass and for which the elimination of the working class is thought of as nothing more than market necessity. Witness the current debate on affordable national health care in the United States. The key factor being considered is not who can access or afford health care but how many millions of people the government can afford to make expendable from the health-care rolls to save costs.

At the national and transnational level, in the Global North and South, the state rules through armed machinery the likes of which have never been seen before. Aída Hernández-Castillo (chapter 6) talks about the links between the Mexican state and organized crime, and Amina Mama (chapter 5) describes the militarized (masculinized, heterosexual) African nation-state as one of the most important targets of engagement for African feminists. These are violent states, yet in the North, specifically in the United States, as we witnessed with the heavily armed police forces overseeing some of the women's marches immediately following the election of Donald Trump, the message communicated to the resisters to explain away the show of force was that the state has to build "security" to protect the homeland. Discourses of "safety of the motherland" mobilized by neoliberal nation-states are profoundly racialized whether they target Black, Brown, or Muslim bodies in the United States or Muslim and Dalit bodies in India. The message is clear and reminds us that this is armed struggle, but only one side is allowed to be armed. Indeed, there is a fundamental difference in the meaning of armed struggle as practiced by the neoliberal state where the primary goal is decimation of the working classes. As Himani Bannerji asserts cogently when speaking of armed resistance in class struggle, "Violence is what the ruling oppressors do; armed struggle is what the resisters do. It would be impossible to make both into the same."

It is in this ultraliberal capitalist moment that Himani speaks of the false ideological notion of "you-can-be-who-you-want-to-be" that undermines any recognition of class struggle. However, our sister-comrades understand that this is what is still taking place as the so-called market forces render more and more of the working classes disposable. Class, together with race and gender, remains the primary factor in the question of social justice. From the persistent police shootings of unarmed Black people to the institutional racism that denies victims' families justice in many of the cases, class struggle remains at the heart of state violence. In the academy the language of class struggle is no longer popular. While discursive change can reformulate ideas for social change, discourse itself does not lead to social change. It is activism that must accompany the ideas that will force such change. Through all the mutations of capitalism, the parameters of social justice have not changed, and thus neither can our commitment to maintaining class struggle.

Building Coalitions and Solidarity across Struggles

Through the intensification of neoliberalism and increasingly militarized state regimes, it follows that the politics of coalition building is even more necessary now than in the past. In earlier periods when our sister-comrades came of age in struggles against the state, oppressed groups came to some shared understanding of their commonalities. Today, however, because of neoliberalism's intense focus on the individual and the market, it is more of a challenge for groups to recognize their commonalities and work to build coalitions and solidarities across common differences. The feminist frameworks that shaped the activism that our sister-comrades speak of here illustrate some of the strongest moments of coalition activism today, most notably in the Movement for Black Lives. This is a coalition that the US state has noted as threatening, and that speaks to the success of the movement forcing the state to reckon with the multiple levels of oppression it forces on all marginalized peoples.

Similarly the State of Israel is threatened by the BDS (Boycott, Divestment, and Sanctions) movement for justice in Palestine, framing it as dangerous and targeting US and European scholar-activists involved in Palestine solidarity work, especially in the academy. As Minnie Bruce Pratt says here, the Black Lives Matter movement teaches us many lessons about solidarity. "Not easily won solidarity, but growing solidarity and a kind of dropping of illusions—the illusions around capitalist democracy, what it is going to give people, and then an opening to ask, 'If that's not working, then what?'" It offers "a lot of questions and desire to talk about other possibilities." In looking at the increasing numbers of people who are being further marginalized by losing their jobs, losing health care, being squeezed by enveloping poverty that forces them to sell personal effects, solidarity pushes people's backs against the wall, and Minnie Bruce asks, "What happens when those people start getting together to push back?" This is a crucial moment in neoliberal capitalism when marginalized communities are beginning to receive the support of many of the not-so-marginalized—those who recognize that the state is a violent and unfair institution that deploys cruelty as a measure of social control.

Thus we recognize with excitement the strength of coalition building that takes the "politics of refusal" Taveeshi Singh refers to in her "Postscript" to a new level: that of solidarity across borders of race, ethnicity, class, gender, and differential abilities. It is the ability of all oppressed groups to see their common struggles that will further strengthen the understanding of the need to come together. Minnie Bruce captures this clearly when she says, "To me, the challenge is more organizational. How does one build, from the ground up, and from that generational gap of people who have been through this struggle before? How does one build those connections to put together some structures that can endure through the kinds of changes that are necessary for people to affirm each other and still stay together in struggle?"

A potential response to this question of solidarity lies in the deeply feminist praxis of conscientization and self-growth in the context of collective struggle. Margo Okazawa-Rey captures this best in chapter 1 when she says, "We as feminists need to develop a methodology that includes a much more conscious way to think about personal growth, personal development, dealing with the contradictions we face in our lives—in the ways in which we have not taken care of each other and of ourselves."

To forge true solidarity, we have to move beyond individual identities and single-issue politics. Margo believes we have to have a collective vision to make struggle meaningful and successful:

> I think about principles, and one of the principles has to be the principle of connectivity—staying connected and moving through various tensions, conflicts, and contradictions in a way where we stay committed to being connected. . . . By connectivity, I mean a

commitment and a practice. Not just a commitment but a practice to work together to understand and dig deeper, to work together to engage conflicts in very generative and creative ways, and to not give up on each other unless it is the absolute last resort.

It is this solidarity that the sister-comrades in this volume speak and practice. As Sara Ahmed says, this is what it means to live "a feminist life."

Wonderful Thinking: On Imagination, Courage, and New Feminist Horizons

Rather than summarizing the radical and inspiring ideas that point to new horizons, we conclude this introduction by quoting at length from each of our sister-comrades. Their words exemplify the courage, critical analysis, hope, and revolutionary feminist praxis that constitute the spirit of this book.

Margo Okazawa-Rey (chapter 1) introduces us to the tools of what she calls "wonderful thinking":

> Engaging in "wonderful thinking" requires us first to create popular-education gatherings—intergenerational, multi-identities, cross-issue, cross-sector—wherever we are located, whenever possible, across geographies. To share local knowledges and personal experiences; to look deeply into and through differences and identities that consistently divide; to apply various critical theoretical perspectives, including socially lived theories; and to generate collective identities, shared structural analyses, and compatible visions of justice, sustainability, and genuine security are radical, potentially transformative acts. . . .
>
> The current political moment, more than ever, demands us to understand, above all, our deepest yearnings.

Angela Y. Davis (chapter 2) pushes this thinking across difference and divides by talking about connectivities among issues and movements, defining how we need to resist:

> The potential success of this resistance will certainly depend on the willingness of organizers and participants to insist on the kind of

intersectional approach to social justice that has been encouraged by antiracist and anticapitalist feminists over the last two decades. It will depend on the recognition, for example, that water is a feminist issue and that our solidarity with the Standing Rock Sioux as they fight to protect their water (and their land and culture) must also be extended to those who live in Flint, Michigan, as well as in Occupied Palestine, who are also fighting for their water, their lives, and their sovereignty.

As we resist, we must never forget why we are resisting.

What we need, then, is a capacious imagination and the ability to create community across social and economic justice struggles.

Minnie Bruce Pratt (chapter 4) thinks deeply about the power of the imagination, including the ways our imaginings have been distorted and truncated by power:

> One of the things I understood as I was doing antiracist work was how profoundly my imagination had been distorted by white supremacy. . . .
>
> So for me, antiracist work has been organizing and being demanding of myself in relation to my writing that I not replicate white supremacy in how I do my work. The only way that has changed . . . is in collective work, in actual on-the-ground work, with people of color, women of color, antiracist white people, people who are opposed to capitalism, opposed to profiting off of other people's labor and bodies.
>
> As I went through that process, my ability to imagine differently was changed, and other possibilities opened up to me. . . . It was not individual imagination that made it happen. It was collective imagination, collective hope, and also the springing from moment to moment of collective work together, so that with each step and each spring forward, another possibility opened up.

Zillah Eisenstein (chapter 7) reflects on honesty and the ethics of antiracist, anti-imperialist coalitions and white feminist allies:

> At this point I trust the world to keep me honest and fully involved in trying to find out what an antiracist, anti-imperialist feminism really looks like. . . .
>
> I wonder what is going to happen for those of us who are committed to an anti-imperial framework. What is going to be our re-

sponsibility here? To do something and to say something. And then also, what is the responsibility of white women within the different women's movements—because we don't have a unified one—in trying to negotiate an honest coalition that asks more than for me to be an ally, that asks for me to be an active participant in the struggle?

Amina Mama (chapter 5), in looking to the future, talks about an "institutional" approach that challenges and transforms oppressive structures at many levels:

> We need to transform institutions, from families through community and government structures, all the way up to global governance structures, so that no terrain is neglected. The plus side of that is that you can be an activist wherever you are. This institutional approach is a different idea of activism, very different from social movement approaches, or revolutionary struggles for state power. In a way, maybe this is something that feminism has contributed to the meaning of politics: a deep understanding of the pervasiveness of power, and its productivity. Resistance to oppression can and does take root in almost any institution, any oppressive situation. It is down to movements to bring things together, so the will to strengthen movements comes from an optimistic viewpoint.

Aída Hernández-Castillo (chapter 6) reflects on the role of scholar-activists and what it means to enter a situation without "the truth":

> With many of these decolonial critiques to ourselves as intellectuals, one issue is that my truth as a feminist of what is emancipation and what is justice is not necessarily what they imagine or what they want. So to arrive to the space of encounter, open to a dialogue in which I am willing to destabilize my certainties, is not as powerful as arriving with "the truth." It is a lot easier to get there with "the truth" than to get there and say, "Well, I just want to see what can we build."

Finally, Himani Bannerji (chapter 3) thinks deeply about what it means that capitalism in its neoliberal phase has created the global crisis–ridden toxic environment that threatens democracy as an emancipatory tool of struggle:

> All aspects of democracy that seem to have become fragile these days must be treasured and fought for. Connections between so-

cial movements ranging over large fields must be mapped up, and solidarity among struggles is critical. Capitalism's expansion into a total socioeconomic and political form requires an equally total network of resistance. It is in this process that we will be able to resolve the relations between race, gender, and class in a political and imaginative manner.

Chapter Structure

Each chapter begins with a section called "Coming of Age" followed by responses to our questions about each scholar-activist's feminist activism and its impact, specific challenges they face in doing this work, their thinking about border crossings and building solidarities, and their vision for the future. Each chapter ends with a section titled "Further Reflections: Imagining a Revolutionary Feminist Politics," focusing on the authors' responses to the following question:

> How would you communicate urgent political and social developments on the horizon in the United States and other parts of the world to generations of younger scholars and activists? We want you to think about this in the context of US political hegemony, the upcoming elections and possible futures; immediate and urgent social justice concerns around migrants, refugees, racism, neoliberal and carceral nation-states, Islamophobia, sexual violence, police brutality, war, occupation, and the rise of misogynist religious fundamentalist movements globally, and also new intersectional movements of resistance like Black Lives Matter and Standing Rock that are located in North America but have had global reverberations.

Our hope is that these stories of Feminist Freedom Warriors inspire and sustain the reader and that they provoke bold, thoughtful, and courageous feminist activism and coalitions in these times, which can often feel more precarious than in the recent past. It is the reason we say, quite seriously, *A Luta Continua!*

No Freedom without Connection

Envisioning Sustainable Feminist Solidarities

Margo Okazawa-Rey

Coming of Age: Margo's Story

Margo Okazawa-Rey: I think I am the classic the-personal-is-political example; by that I mean I started my life journey in a transnational context, in a sense, by the way my parents met. My father was part of the US occupying force in post–World War II Japan, working-class, a conscript for the "war effort"; my mother was part of the occupied, upper-middle class, the college-educated daughter of Japanese corporate executive. My own birth signifies, or I personify, something that was not supposed to exist at that historical moment.

So in my life I've had to figure out questions of identity and place. There was a time when I just really wanted to fit in. This was before I came out. I tried to fit in racially and in terms of gender, but when I came out as a lesbian, I thought, "Oh, my god, there's not going to be one place where I am going to fit."

Chandra Talpade Mohanty: When was that? How old were you?

MOR: I was twenty-four. I had just finished my masters. After a couple of years of trying to coming out and all that stuff, I realized the thing to do is to help create places for people who, according to established categories, "don't fit." So my feminism and politics really did grow out of a personal place of figuring out a place for me.

Linda E. Carty: And where was the place that happened?

MOR: The geographic place was Boston. Boston, Cambridge, in 1972 was quite a place. I met lots of other feminists—feminists of color, white women, and a whole generation of us were going through that journey, of who we are, what our politics are. It was a very exciting time, because there were so many ideas that we were trying to explore, like monogamy, non-monogamy, and even little bits around transgender stuff. We tried living collectively. Through all of these kinds of social experiments I learned a lot, to say the least. One of the things I learned and became clear about was my politics. Also became clearer about my ethics and values and what really mattered. That was almost a ten-year journey, from 1972 to 1982. That was the personal part, but it was very much connected to the political.

My politics are deeply rooted in what I notice around me, as well as what I'm reading, the conversations I'm having with people. But they are not abstract; they are not theoretical, in a kind of a classic sense. They are theoretical in a feminist theoretical sense—theorizing from lived experience, then putting that together with things I'm learning through reading and conversations with folks like you. So I feel very grounded and steady as I'm growing in what I think, how

I think, and where I have landed at this point of my life. So the first point has to do with the situation I was born into and the events and forces in the political moment and geographic location that politicized me. Much, much later, a crucial turning point for me was doing the Fulbright research fellowship to South Korea. That is where I really began to think about and experience the category of nation. When you're in a dominant category, you don't really think about it until you have a contrasting experience. That's one of the "invisible privileges" of having a US citizenship.

CTM: When was that?

MOR: That was 1994. Before then I had been active in various activist projects, and I was a member of the Combahee River Collective before we named ourselves Combahee River Collective.[1] In winter of 1975 I met up with this group of Black feminists. I can't remember how I got connected to them. We used to meet in one of our members' living rooms—Helen Stewart. At that time there were maybe five of us meeting together. The ages ranged from twenty, who we considered the baby of the group, and the oldest person was Helen. I think she was twenty-six or twenty-seven. We were young, and we were just trying to explain our lives, really. Many of us were lesbian—not all; some were bisexual. We were active in lots of different projects and struggles and just trying to figure out our place in our communities as Black women, as Black lesbians, as socialists, feminists, and anti-imperialists. We were not setting out to make history. We simply were trying to explain our lives and theorizing about what was going on around us and our place in it. It's kind of a shock to me every time I hear the Combahee River Statement referenced as an important touchstone for younger generations of feminists and people are doing dissertations about Combahee in one way or another.

CTM: What makes the Combahee River Collective statement powerful is that it is so explicitly socialist and anticapitalist. There aren't that many examples of those kinds of connections being made that include a very central critique of capitalism.

MOR: Yes, exactly. I get so upset when these days many feminists in the academy and other places have reduced intersectionality down to multiple identities, because that was just one strand of how we saw the intersections. There was absolutely an anti-imperialist, materialist analysis. My goal now is to really push back and say, "You can't do intersectionality without looking at those two or three other strands."

LEC: There is a particular kind of history and a particular kind of materiality attached to that history that locates women of color in specific places, particularly in US capitalism. If we don't understand that, then what is intersectionality? Nothing but identities.

MOR: Yes, exactly. I absolutely detest it. I want to go on record saying that. Let's go back a bit. I went to Korea as a Fulbright scholar. My proposal was to try to understand what Korean people thought of African American people before they arrived in the US, because this was a time when there were serious tensions and violence between Korean merchants and African American communities. There was the big Red Apple incident in New York,[2] LaTasha Harlins in LA,[3] there was stuff in Boston. Everywhere, everywhere. I was living in Washington at the time and had helped found a group called the Afro-Asian Relations Council, trying to bring together the two groups. I thought, "Well, they couldn't have just come here clean slate. They had to have some ideas and opinions about Black people in the US." So I went with that as the starting place, but I actually ended up looking at the extensive presence of US bases. At the time there were over a hundred bases and installations in South Korea, which is about one-fourth the size of California. I was shocked. There were lots of military personnel. There's a base right in the middle of Seoul. Although I did not speak Korean, I spoke Japanese, and the way I could communicate with many of the Korean people of a particular generation was through Japanese. That was because of the Japanese colonization of Korea.

So here I am, in the middle of Seoul, having the US passport and speaking Japanese, and finding myself connected to these two imperial nations that had and is having such an impact on Korea. Because of how I look—pretty ambiguous—people couldn't figure me out. I remember being in a phone booth, trying to make a phone call, and somebody taps on the window and asks me in very rough English, "Are you Filipina?" and I said, "No." On this one day, and all the time I was there were these kinds of micro things happening, and all the macro and global things happening right in the middle of Seoul. I can look backwards and see my location much better than I could when I was there. So by getting a sense of the importance of "nation," looking at militarism, looking at my own origin in a military context, and looking at Korea, and then through my friend Gwyn [Kirk] making the connections of the bases in the Philippines, Korea, Okinawa, and Japan is how we launched the International Women's Network against Militarism.[4] It started as East Asia–US Women's Network against US Militarism in 1997.[5] That brought in the East Asian countries with US military presence as well as the US. Being part of creating the network is another example of being in a particular situation and trying to make sense of it and then something coming out of that.

CTM: Right, but it is more than also just being in a particular situation. From what I'm hearing from you, it's also about how you anchor yourself and your identity and your politics and your questions in that particular space so that there are connections between the intellectual, political questions you take on and your own life as you see it.

MOR: That is a lovely way to put it.

LEC: In some ways you are the embodiment of all those intersections and contradictions. It helps you to really understand them, not only as an outsider within, like when you are in Korea, but as an insider without, as Japanese, as relating to the coloniality of Japan and Korea/the

US and Korea, as you were saying before. It brings them to a center for you that makes complete sense to you individually.

MOR: Yes, and what you are saying is really a good way to talk about what my mother said to me, in a very concrete way. This was when I was very young, living in Japan, and there were some kids who were teasing me. I said to my mom, "Am I Japanese?" and she said, "Yes, you are absolutely Japanese, but that can be mostly inside the house, and when you go outside, people are going to see you as Black." I don't know how she knew that, but that's exactly what you're getting to. She gave me the permission to be both, but also to contextualize it, which was a very important early lesson.

LEC: A lesson in self-empowerment, because she is giving you permission to be.

MOR: Yes, and she must have understood it on some level for herself as well.

CTM: It is a very concrete way to understand multiple identities—that they are not multiple in the sense of one plus one plus one, but they are multiple in the sense of the layers that we live, that are relevant at all moments of our lives. You may be Japanese indoors, but you are also African American.

MOR: It depends on the context. Those glass jars that have multicolored layered sand? They're different colors, but they're not layered absolutely horizontally. You can see the ways that the sand settles, and if you shake it up, you get a different image.

CTM: Nice image about multiplicity. Sometimes the way we talk about those things, we separate stuff. It's difficult to talk about intersectionality and multiplicity in dynamic ways, and this is a very dynamic image of shifts.

MOR: I think that's how I experience my life. Things change a lot. Certain things always remain. They get moved to different places, depending on where I am. It is through my work with the network where I really began to understand what transnational feminist praxis is about, and the core of it is building strong relationships. It is the sturdy connections that keep the network going. It's not just the tasks. Of course we are about the various activities and actions, but over the years—now the network is going on twenty years—it is the quality of the relationships among the members. There's a core group of us in all the countries, and it's those relationships that have really carried the day. For example, I just came back from Gwyn's seventieth birthday party, and every country group sent something talking about the impact she's had on their lives and the network.

CTM: It must have been so moving.

MOR: It was very moving, because in the moment you're not thinking about what impact are you going to make; you're just fully present, engaging, doing the work, being human, being feminist. Looking back, all of these things are brought forward, so to speak, and you are reminded that you don't necessarily think about what impact you're having in the moment.

CTM: How did this lead you to Palestine?

MOR: There was a conference in 2003, called "Womanoeuvres: Feminist Debates on Peace and Security." It was in Zurich. A friend of mine named Malathi de Alwis,[6] a Sri Lankan feminist whom I had met in another context, emailed me and said, look, there is a conference going on, and there is nothing from Asia, maybe you should send them something. So, uncharacteristically forward, I did. I sent them an email and said, "Maybe I can contribute something about Asia," and immediately they replied, and I ended up there. It was just an amazing experience. One of the highlights, of course, was meeting my friend, the late Maha Abu-Dayyeh.[7] I gave a keynote and she gave a keynote, then we ended up in a workshop together, where she and Cynthia Cockburn were talking about women living under occupation and militarism and I was in the audience.[8] We got to know each other through that conference, then about a year and a half later she invited me to come to help start the research and documentation unit at her organization, the Women's Centre for Legal Aid and Counselling in Ramallah and Jerusalem at the time.[9] I just couldn't believe it, and of course I went. When things come up so serendipitously, I always jump at it and then see what's in store for me. That was exactly ten years ago.

Similar to my time in South Korea, I started thinking about what it means to be connected to the US, as part of an occupying force, and my country, the USA, being a supporter and the foundation of the occupation—economic, political, and ideological. And what it means to be in Ramallah or the West Bank, more broadly, or occupied East Jerusalem, and doing the work I'm doing, and asking questions about what is my role there. I was invited there. I didn't just barge in or go on a tourist adventure, but it still raises those questions. What is my role, what is my responsibility, and how do I enter into those places? Ten years later I can say with all humility that it's about the quality of the relationships—of going in, unassuming, and absolutely showing up and actually being of service, in whatever ways I could. And then, the other side of that is seeing the disconnect between academics and the NGO [nongovernmental organization] folks. I was very in the swim with the NGO people, and less connected with the academics. One of the reasons I was brought in is there was a sense, among staff at the center as well as Maha, that the academics do what academics often do: gather the data, use the knowledge of those at the center, and then not really give them credit, or not be very service-oriented. In Palestine it's very specific, because everybody knows each other, and there's a history of struggle, but at the same time there's still a structural divide.

I remember having a conversation with one academic, at Birzeit [University], and she was asking me what kind of research I was teaching. I said, "Well, I come from the perspective of feminist research methodologies and really honoring women's experiences, and so it tends to be qualitative." And she was so adamant and said, "That's going to get you nowhere, and that's not going to show you anything." I was shocked at the vehemence with which she came back at me. I said, "Well, I disagree with you, and it seems that the ways that we're talking about research at the center resonate with the staff and the volunteers who are working with us. So let's just agree to disagree." I saw her when I was at Maha's funeral, and she was very emotional with me, not just about the passing of Maha. I inferred from that that maybe she had some second thoughts.

CTM: I am thinking about how you conceptualize being a feminist and what it means for you to live a feminist life. Some of what you described is very much about a deep understanding of living a particular kind of life, being of service in a particular way, understanding the world in a certain way.

MOR: What feminism is about, I think, is absolutely centering the lives of women, and that of course by definition, then, you understand other people—children, girls, boys, men, transgender people—as well. Recognizing the ways in which women's lives are affected in particular ways by the various forces that affect women in specific locations—economic globalization, militarism, and religious fundamentalisms, for example. There are also certain common threads that, being transnational in the ways I have talked about, help me see the connections without being reductionist. So for me feminism is a materialist feminism, an anti-imperialist feminism, an intersectional feminism that pulls in all those forces and institutional arrangements that enable us to see that women's lives are affected in very profound ways, from micro to global levels of analysis. It is centrally about looking at and improving the lives of women and recognizing that we share a common destiny, even though the particularities obviously are very different.

LEC: Right, and you see that is what is so fundamental about this kind of feminism. Listening to you talk about your life, it doesn't have any kind of linear structural thinking around what do we theorize about feminism and how do we live it. I hear quite clearly that feminism is the lived experience and understanding the impact of what you do on women's lives. And as that changes, then you move with it, because there can't be stasis, but you're seeing the impact on women's lives, and that is impacting you at the same time.

CTM: Which is different from having an academic area of expertise and then just staying within the boundaries of that area of expertise.

LEC: Not being able to move outside of it, because there is no pragmatism to that, and there is no investment in anything else. So this lived experience is separate from that. People who do that can't understand and appreciate what's going on in women's lives. What do we need to do to make a better tomorrow for all of us? Like when you go to Palestine and have that kind of experience, it's forcing you to think, "Something is wrong with this kind of capitalism that is going on in my country, that is impacting these women's lives in this horrible kind of way." It brings a different kind of understanding of what we need to create, and what really needs to happen, that makes this grounded feminism.

MOR: Yeah. The title of Gwyn Kirk's and my intro to the women's studies textbook is *Women's Lives*,[10] and it follows women's lives, as I'm living my own life, and there are new realizations and new insights all the time as I build on what I have already studied or what I am already familiar with. It is a kind of theoretical dynamism. I don't want to make it too grand, but you get the idea. And that to me is what makes being this kind of feminist really enlivening, energizing, and for me the core of it is about a love that is big and foundational and so essential to the relationships that I spoke about earlier—to vision. It all comes together for me around that.

CTM: Tell us a little bit about some of the difficult moments or challenges you've faced in doing this kind of work, with all the different communities of people you have been working with over the years.

MOR: Confronting my own limitations, then embracing them at the same time so I can grow; figuring out how to face that kind of vulnerability; not knowing, when I think I should know something. Kind of bumping up against myself. Another one, especially in relation to Palestine, is explaining to people what it is I'm doing but not having the words to do it. This is, one, because people don't really get Palestine, even though they might know it in their minds, or they have images of it. So they ask, "What are you doing there?" and I start talking, and people's eyes glaze over or their pupils dilate, and I think I have lost them somehow. I think about that as both the real challenge but also a metaphorical one. What happens when I'm trying to explain something, whether it's there or here, when some things just aren't very explainable and there are not necessarily words?

Part of not having the words is maybe I'm not understanding something clearly enough that I can put it in words, or there simply may not be words. So I've started learning filmmaking to try and see if I can get a little creative. I think the other really hard thing is trying to be in two places at once. It is absolutely impossible. I can't be here in the States, or in Berkeley, where I live, and be in Palestine. So wherever I am, I almost have to let it go, in a funny way, to keep it together, to stay connected. At the same time now, I am just figuring out how to stay connected to my colleagues and close friends in Palestine, some of whom now claim me as family member living in America. I signed up for this thing where you can send video emails. A lot of times I send messages like "Hi, it's me! I've been thinking about you." My experiences in Palestine really brought home that there is no freedom without connection and there is no connection without freedom. You can't just be free; you end up just being a helium balloon and you are going to run out of air. Or if there is no freedom, you are just connected, then you are going to suffocate. It's hard to figure out that balance between freedom and connection.

LEC: Don't you think part of the glazed-over look people get in their eyes when you talk about Palestine has something to do with not just a basic lack of understanding, but lack of interest and connection to the Other? Because this is an Other that has been connected in this country, in particular kinds of negative ways, in very violent ways, and there is no connection to that Other. As I am listening to you, I am thinking about Haiti. It happens with Haiti all the time. I have done a lot of work in Haiti, and so I know the disconnect. You see it and feel it—"Oh, those people again, over there." So what is it that gives you a different kind of seeing and knowing than they can ever imagine, which prevents them from connecting too?

MOR: Yes, I do. I was thinking, too, that being there and living there I got to experience lots of things that you wouldn't necessarily if you were just visiting. And when I was living there those three years, I would sometimes go to Switzerland for meetings, and I remember I went to get massages, and I remember the massage therapist saying, "Wow, you're carrying all this tension." I had lots of mobility because I'm not Palestinian, but there are ways in which just being in that space and going through the daily checkpoint experience, or the experience of my being around colleagues who lost family, there is this secondary impact that I just didn't realize.

LEC: How would you say the challenges that you have encountered over the years have impacted the goals and outcomes that you initially envisioned when you started?

MOR: One challenge that I didn't mention yet is the challenge of building institutions and how much energy and vision and effort and time and work it takes to create those institutions, and then how quickly they can fall apart, implode, from the weight of contradictions or some internal discord, not just external forces setting out to destroy it. Most recently I've been thinking about the challenge of creating institutions that are solid, that are responsive and can withhold or withstand earthquakes, metaphorically speaking, and that breathe and continue to develop and grow as the material and political conditions change. Having said that, I think another challenge is knowing when to let institutions go and how to end institutions gracefully, with dignity, and recognizing that it is time for this formation to end and then move to something else. That requires a certain kind of redefined leadership so that the power and the position can be flexible with the changes that need to take place.

LEC: We have all been in organizing for so many years. We know the implosions you are talking about can't be prevented. How do you think these implosions can be managed in more strategic ways so that the organization can continue without falling apart?

MOR: We as feminists need to develop a methodology that includes a much more conscious way to think about personal growth, personal development, dealing with the contradictions we face in our lives—in the ways in which we haven't taken care of each other and of ourselves, in a way that we can deal with whatever traumatic experiences we've had, or betrayals, or the negative experiences we've had as activists or in the academy—so that we're not taking it out on each other, which is often. What kind of methodology will help us do the work, become conscious, do the healing as we're doing the work? Let's say, for example, we go to therapy. Well, we see the therapeutic is really being separated from the intellectual or the activist part. What kind of methodology will really help us bring all of those parts together and do it in a conscious and purposeful way?

CTM: Do you think this means some way of reenvisioning the feminist self? What that might mean in terms of relationships with other people . . . other feminists?

MOR: Yes.

LEC: Even though in that reenvisioning we understand that there is no uniformity to the feminist self. But there's a required feminist consciousness for whatever form reenvisioning takes that makes us at least sensitive to each other so that we can work together.

MOR: Right, and the way I envision that is to think about the idea that there is no "I" without "you"; that I am "I" and you are "you," but the definition and the construction happen together. It's really interesting that in Western psychology, pathology is codependence, and in Eastern thought, pathology is when you become too separated from others, the collective. It seems to me that we really need to figure out the relationship between the two—the separation and the togetherness, the individual and collective. As I mentioned before, I have come to recognize from all my travels and being in very different places that there is no connection without freedom and there is no freedom without connection. How do we put that principle in place as we are doing the work? The intellectual work, the activist work.

CTM: That seems particularly poignant right now in terms of the kinds of divides around race, class, nationality, sexuality, ability, within a culture of neoliberalism, which has its own specific kind of impact on how people see themselves, and how our relationship to institutions, to organizing, to complicity, to all of these ways of thinking, about even what freedom means, are impacted.

MOR: Yes, absolutely right. I would add that it's not just in the context of neoliberalism but also in the context of a hyper-individualist way of being in the world that is encouraged and rewarded. It is a bedrock of mainstream US culture, but it seems to be taking hold in other places as well. The context of oppression necessarily means the appropriation of identity and agency and how to reclaim all of those things without having it being an individualist, self-absorbed kind of identity. It means not operating out of a politics of scarcity that says there's not enough status, there's not enough power, and whatever it is, we're not going to share. It's not a collective way to think about power and status.

CTM: How do you build solidarity in the face of all these things?

MOR: I like your idea of the common context of struggle.[11] I think there's the context, but I think there are also principles around which we build solidarities. We are talking about particular ways we struggle around various issues, but it can't just be struggle around issues; it also has to be a generative struggle around vision. It can't just be identities, although identities obviously are important. Particularly in the US, we have gotten bogged down into a very specific way to think about identities. It is sometimes very essentialist. It is also very individualist. Even though we talk group, I think we are often referring to ourselves—*my* identity and so on. I think about principles, and one of the principles has to be the principle of connectivity—staying connected and moving through various tensions, conflicts, and contradictions in a way where we stay committed to being connected. And by that I mean that we are not going to give up on each other unless it is absolutely necessary. By connectivity, I mean a commitment *and* a practice. Not just a commitment but a practice to work together to understand and dig deeper, to work together to engage conflicts in very generative and creative ways, and to not give up on each other unless it is the absolute last resort. Even then, giving up, to me, doesn't mean that that person, or those people, or that group may not have another chance. It's in the moment we say, "Okay, we need to let this go; maybe we'll come back to it."

Another kind of connectivity is connecting to our environment, the physical environment, and remembering that we share a common destiny not only with human beings but with the natural environment as well. What kind of practice will help us remember that and stay connected? I think another important principle is thinking about creativity and redefining resources, because, as we've talked about before, capitalism and neoliberalism have really shaped what we value as a society, and many parts of the world too; thinking about the material and the consumer, about the worth and value, of each other and of ideas, and of the ways we're committed. There is something profoundly valuable about ideas and about vision, and that they are not just mechanical, technical things that we try to generate, but they are creativity, for example, and generations of ideas and new knowledges.

CTM: Also perhaps based on connectivity and not extraction.

MOR: Yes, exactly! That we're not extracting ideas and resources from human beings or from the environment, but that with true connectivity we're able to generate ideas, ways of doing, ways of being in the wider world. I envision a new society or different society where there are lots of free spaces, where the visioning, the creativity, the activism can happen in a way that can be ongoing. We're thinking about seven generations, not just our generation or the next generation, where I can see us dancing, laughing, and playing and being creative. We're also engaging in struggle because there are always new contradictions and we have to be prepared. I don't see the new society as this clean place and that's the end of it.

LEC: In envisioning this new world, and considering the current generations, what do you see in the future of feminism, particularly among women of color?

MOR: At the risk of sounding like a Luddite or a dinosaur, I think some of the principles of feminism that have shaped me will apply for a while. One of those principles is understanding power and all the various ways in which power—interpersonal, structural, institutional—is made manifest and operates consciously, unconsciously, and subliminally. One of the things that feminism has done is help us think about power and particularly its impact on women. And here I want to say "women," as well as the broader category of "gender," because I'm most specially interested in the lives of women, and having done lots of work in various parts of the world, it's a very important category that shapes people's experiences. So I don't want to lose that. I want to stay committed to that. I think we have lost it a little bit by saying "feminisms." I think there is "feminism" and there are various ways that women and people around the world practice it. I think the essential part of feminism that I want to retain is the understanding of power at all the levels that I just mentioned, and the connectivity. I definitely think transnational feminism is important—intersectionality, all those things—but it would be a mistake to lose the essence of it.

Further Reflections:
Imagining a Revolutionary Feminist Politics

MOR: Bernice Johnson Reagon has a lyric that goes "We who believe in freedom cannot rest until it comes."[12] We've been there. Done that. Will do it again, and again, and again. We will until we have transformed the material conditions; people's consciousness; and political, economic, and sociocultural processes that produced the election of the new fascist, unabashedly pro-capital, antilife US president; that may bring far-right National Front to power in France; that buttress right-wing regimes worldwide. The current political turn is neither new nor unique in the US and elsewhere. Capitalism, militarism, and religious fundamentalism, entwined with patriarchy and misogyny, ethnic and racial supremacy, and accumulated phobias, constitute the bedrock of the world order in which we exist.

In such a world, one liberation does not guarantee liberation of all. For example, in Nobel Peace Prize winner Aung San Suu Kyi's newly "democratized" Myanmar. Just one year later, the military are reportedly killing adults and children, raping women and girls, pillaging and burning down villages, and committing other atrocities against the Muslim Ruáingga (Rohingya) people living on the border of Bangladesh. According to Amnesty International, "While the military bears ultimate responsibility for the violations, State Counsellor Aung San Suu Kyi—the de facto head of Myanmar's civilian government—has failed in her political and moral responsibility to speak out."[13] What lessons about leading political struggles, forming movements, considering change methodologies, and "post-struggle" conditions must movement folks draw from examples like Myanmar, among others? What can we apply to US struggles and movements?

Septima Clark said, "I have great belief in the fact that whenever there is chaos, it creates wonderful thinking. I consider chaos a gift."[14] Chaos is one way to describe the current political moment and, I too, consider it a gift of possibilities and transformation. However, chaos often creates more chaos and generates fear, greed, and hoarding, and a politics of scarcity rather than collective approaches to what faces us, even among progressive scholars and activists. The current chaos requires both urgent actions to resist the many frontal assaults we face as well as visioning, longer-term strategizing, and transforming the deeply internalized, often unconscious, oppression and domination, as we also have been systematically socialized across generations in a society marked by inequalities and all forms of oppression.

Engaging in "wonderful thinking" requires us first to create popular-education gatherings—intergenerational, multi-identities, cross-issue, cross-sector—wherever we are located and, whenever possible, across geographies. To share local knowledges and personal experiences; to look deeply into and through differences and identities that consistently divide; to apply various critical theoretical perspectives, including socially lived theories; and to generate collective identities, shared structural analyses, and compatible visions of justice, sustainability, and genuine security are radical, potentially transformative acts.

Asking, "Why did 'they' vote for Trump? What do we do now?" only to repeat the already monotonous answers will lead us to places not much different from where we are now, and, more important, these questions tie us to the very problems we want to address. Wonderful thinking includes, most fundamentally, understanding, not simply knowing:

> Knowing . . . refers to factual information or the process by which it is gathered. Understanding . . . refers to systematically grasping the significance of an event in such a way that it becomes integrated into one's moral and intellectual life. . . . Facts can be absorbed without their having any impact on how we understand ourselves or the world we live in. Facts in themselves do not make a difference; it is the understanding of them that makes the difference.[15]

The current political moment, more than ever, demands us to understand, above all, our deepest yearnings. We must somehow reach individually and collectively into souls—of "our" people and us and our "Other"—to excavate those lodged deep within, intergenerations of yearnings buried under layers of histories, pain, and confusion. Unexpressed for myriad reasons, from being out of words, to fear, to mistrust of others' willingness to hear, understand, and affirm. Unspoken because of our certainty, unconscious perhaps, that yearning is somehow a frivolous and "unproductive" activity.

What could we come to understand if we discovered the deepest yearnings that led the US electorate to vote for their candidate or not vote at all? What could we come to understand if we discovered the deepest yearnings of immigrants and refugees? Of incarcerated peoples? Of survivors of violence? Of activists and scholars struggling for change?

Anne Braden said, "In every age, no matter how cruel the oppression carried on by those in power, there have been those who struggled for a different world. I believe this is the genius of humankind, the thing that makes us half divine: the fact that some human beings can envision a world that has never existed."[16]

I am convinced that uncovering and affirming our deepest collective yearnings will prevent us from dedicating ourselves to the liberation only of particular peoples and not others, the crudest form of identity politics. Collective yearnings are one of our life forces, so instead [they] will motivate and inspire us to envision the world that has yet to exist. And when we can imagine, we can also be creative in how we "do" change work.

As Grace Lee Boggs once stated, "A revolution that is based on the people exercising their creativity in the midst of devastation is one of the great historical contributions of humankind."[17] That is the revolution to which we must dedicate ourselves.

Troubling Explanatory Frameworks

Feminist Praxis across Generations

Angela Y. Davis

Coming of Age: Angela's Story

Angela Y. Davis: It's kind of a complicated story because it took me awhile to begin to positively and critically identify with feminism, even though as I look back now, I have been doing feminist activism for a long time. In the late 1960s, when I was doing work on women's rights and Black women and a whole range of issues, like International Women's Day, I considered feminism to be bourgeois—white and bourgeois. So I did not identify with feminism. As a matter of fact, when I wrote *Women, Race, and Class*, I was kind of shocked that everybody began to refer to it as feminist: "No, no, no, no, I'm a communist! I'm a Black woman revolutionary, and that would be oxymoronic!"[1] But as women-of-color feminism began to develop, I began to quite comfortably identify with that feminism. I suppose I had to recognize that there are different feminisms, multiple feminisms, and there are some feminisms with which I still absolutely hesitate to identify.

Chandra Talpade Mohanty: Whom would you identify as the women-of-color feminist voices that felt the most like a space that you could interact with at that time? You are talking about the late seventies to early eighties now?

AYD: Yes. Well, I was fortunate to be able to hang out with people like bell hooks and Cherríe Moraga and Gloria Anzaldúa. For me 1981 is the pivotal year. *This Bridge Called My Back* was published,[2] bell hooks's book was published.[3] In that year, I think, my own book was published. Around the same time, Michele Wallace's book was published.[4]

CTM: Yeah, Michele Wallace's book, and Gloria Joseph and Jill Lewis's *Common Differences.*[5]

AYD: Yes, exactly. And then there were these amazing conferences that took place: "Common Differences,"[6] "Parallels and Intersections."[7] So it wasn't as if I had to make an effort. The scene was already set. The framework came together. I was held by it, so to speak. I was teaching at San Francisco State at that time, and so were Cherríe Moraga,[8] Gloria,[9] and bell hooks,[10] and around that time new formations were happening. There were amazing confrontations at various conferences, for example, at the NWSA.[11] I did not attend the one in 1981, which was in Storrs [Connecticut], but I did attend the conference the following year. I went to the one at Humboldt State, in Arcata [California]. The theme was around racism, but there were major issues there. That, I think, was such a productive, generative period. I was teaching in women's studies. I had not actually thought of myself as a person who fit into the new field of women's studies. I felt a greater kinship with Black studies. At that particular time I wasn't interested in a full-time academic career, because I was doing a great deal of activism—traveling and speaking and organizing, I wanted to continue that. So I got this offer from San Francisco State to teach in the relatively new women's studies department and at the same time, as I mentioned, bell hooks was teaching there. I don't think they realized what was going on.

CTM: It is incredible to think that you, Cherríe, Gloria, and bell hooks were in the same space at that time. I never knew that, actually.

Linda E. Carty: That was a radical space then.

AYD: But it was a contested space as well, because I can remember the difficulties I had teaching courses in the women's studies department. I would be told this is not appropriate for women's studies; this is more appropriate for Black studies. I remember very specifically an encounter with a faculty member with whom I was co-teaching the introductory course. At that particular time I was thinking about the book that I would write later, on the blues: *Blues Legacies and Black Feminism.*[12] We had this huge fight in front of the students about the blues when this white woman faculty member was telling me that this was entirely inappropriate for a women's studies class because the blues were all about men beating up women and so forth and so on. For me that was a pivotal moment, when I realized how much work would have to be done within that field. I guess the work is still happening.

CTM: And needs to happen still. I was curious about your socialist commitments and how that plays out in women-of-color feminism. Because I don't think there were too many people who identified as such in women's studies at that time.

AYD: Oh, but then that was the era of socialist feminism. You have people like Zillah [Eisenstein],[13] her amazing book.

CTM: Yes, there is a genealogy.

AYD: I came to my work on gender though my socialist, communist trajectory. I read *Origin of the Family, Private Property, and the State* long before there had been any discussion of the field of women's studies.[14]

LEC: I hear that thing you are saying about the contestation, because if you look at the literature back then, you see the point of contestation. The theoretical foundation of understanding social relations in capitalism was not happening in feminism. It was not happening in women's studies. That is where I would see you being on the outside as the communist looking in from a socialist feminist frame at what's not happening in the field at that time.

CTM: So you are talking about the institutionalized aspects of women's and gender studies. That is what the distinction is. When women's studies get institutionalized, there are almost no spaces that I can think of where there is a socialist feminist orientation to the field. There are socialist feminist theorists and activists in the world, producing those knowledges. I know this because I remember some of the same struggles not just around race and US exceptionalism but also class. The analysis of social relations was very fundamentally anticapitalist. And that's from the point of view of somebody who has been in women's studies, so through the institutional lens.

AYD: But I think there were some, certain figures around whom—

CTM: Socialist feminists—

AYD: Yes. I'm thinking about UC–Santa Cruz and the department I came to teach in for many years—the History of Consciousness. When that program was founded, it was around socialist feminism, so at a certain point there was a far too simplistic assumption of what it meant to do work around gender or around women's issues. Some of this came from the communist framework as well—the woman question—which is how I came to it. And I had to figure out how to extricate myself from the framework without leaving behind what was productive and what was important. But I think as women's studies came to be institutionalized, it gave rise to a whole strain of literature that moved away from engagement with issues of class and imperialism. I actually like to think about what was happening on the ground in communities outside of the academy, and if I think about the work that women of color were doing, I am thinking specifically about a genealogy that goes back to people like Fran Beal, [who] back in 1970 published that amazing piece "Double Jeopardy: To Be Black and Female,"[15] and then [there was] the Third World Women's Alliance that developed this framework. The name of their newspaper was *Triple Jeopardy*.

Today when people refer to "intersectionality" as if that category had always been around, it has been so completely naturalized now that they don't take into consideration that much of the impetus for developing a framework that was capable of addressing these issues together came directly from people, women especially, working on the ground, doing activism against war, activism within the labor movement, activism against, for example, sterilization abuse. "Triple jeopardy" referred to racism, sexism, and imperialism; those were the three categories, and, of course, imperialism embraced capitalism. I felt drawn to that analysis all along but did not necessarily see it as feminist. It was the alternative framework to what was then considered to be feminism, and it was that framework that didn't make it into the academy and would take another ten years before it became available, and then perhaps not until—well, it hasn't really made it into some departments. It still has not in 2016. It's really important to look at all of the ways in which the work outside of the academy had a direct impact on what would eventually be taken up within.

LEC: So in reflecting on your feminist and activist work over the last four decades, how do you imagine that work has impacted the lives of women? How do you see it moving through the lives of women in real ways and creating change? And this is, of course, in the imaginary, because some of it you will know for sure and some you would hope that it does.

AYD: Well, I think that whenever one engages in work that is designed to contribute to social transformation, one only hopes to have an impact. For me, I have never imagined that impact has been confined to the work that I do as an individual. I always see it as a collective process. Even things that I have done, like the book that I wrote in 1981, *Women, Race, and Class*, a lot of those ideas came from my activism and came from my community. So when people tell me that they were profoundly transformed by that, I can't take the credit for it myself. I suppose I would say that I always hope to be connected to communities that have some impact on the world, that make a difference in the world, that make it perhaps somewhat easier to move forward. And, of course, change is never a given. What can be a very positive transformation at one point can turn into its opposite so easily. I don't think it's a good thing to rest on one's laurels, because we can see that some victories within the academy, departments, fields that seem so revolutionary at the time—

CTM: Are completely co-opted.

AYD: Exactly. So I think it is always important to look back and understand the histories and the genealogies, but at the same time it is important to look forward and not say, "Oh! This is what I have done and I feel proud of what I have done."

CTM: If you were to specify the issues, concerns, contradictions that really engaged you, within which you had worked over this long period of time, what would those spaces be?

AYD: Well, I think I have always been interested in complicating whatever is given. I can even remember when I was young and I felt drawn to communism, I joined a communist youth organization when I was in my teens, and that was a decision I made even though my parents had many friends who were communists. I can remember I instinctively felt that racism and class exploitation had to be thought of together, so that it wasn't only a class analysis that overshadowed everything else. It was about breaking down hierarchies of the understanding of the way oppression works in the world. Later, when I was a member of the Communist Party and I was active in the Black Panther Party, those of us who were in other parties were told that we had to choose whether we wanted to remain in the Black Panther Party or pick the other party. That wasn't a difficult decision for me. As passionate as I felt about the work in Black communities and the work I was doing with the Black Panther Party, I needed a larger framework. My experiences within the Communist Party gave me this global framework, this way of identifying not only with labor struggles and struggles that were being conducted by people of other racial and ethnic backgrounds, white workers, and so forth, but also the world. I am still talking about that today, because even as we are witnessing a new flourishing of activism today, there could be a more pronounced internationalism, but in the United States of America we are always encouraged to look inward and not outward.

LEC: A problem of insularity.

CTM: If you were to think concretely about what we face now, what are some of the most urgent challenges that we face in doing serious, radical feminist, antiracist, anti-imperialist praxis?

AYD: In some ways we really missed the boat on a whole number of issues. I say this not to be overly critical, but because it is important to take promises that were unfulfilled in the past and use them to help us to build agendas for the present. So I can remember back in the seventies when we first began to talk about violence against women, I wrote a piece for Kitchen Table Press on violence against women.[16] It was called *Violence against Women and the Ongoing Challenge to Racism.*[17] I can't remember what year it was, but I do remember in the seventies taking up this issue in relation to the Joan Little case. That,

I know, was seventy-five or seventy-six. Joan Little, of course, was a young Black woman who was raped by a guard in a prison in North Carolina. I wrote a piece for *Ms.* magazine, and I remember that we were talking at that time about the importance of men getting involved in the campaign against violence against women. There was an organization called Black Men Against Rape, and a number of small formations of men who had taken up the issue of combating gender— what we called then "violence against women." This, I think, may have been in the early eighties in Washington, DC. I remember thinking back then that this is what needs to be done, this is how we're actually going to eradicate gender violence. But it didn't catch on.

There were a few men's groups here and there who were doing that work, but it wasn't embraced. That means that here we are in the sixteenth year of the twenty-first century, and that's still on the agenda. So that is one of the main challenges, and I am very happy to see young men, young Black men especially, taking up feminist frameworks. I have encountered groups of young students here and there, men doing work in rape crisis centers, women's centers, and in this new student activism. I think it is very much shaped by feminism, and that has to do with Black Lives Matter and the activist feminist framework that has become a part of activism today. I don't think it is possible for young people to consider themselves serious activists if they don't embrace feminism to a certain extent. So it is both, a challenge, but I see some real hopeful developments.

LEC: You just pointed to what has been missing and the kinds of mistakes that we have all made and contributed to. Thinking back on that, what do you think needs to happen in terms of feminists across race, ethnic, class divides and national borders to build solidarity, to really have an understanding of how to contribute to necessary change in this age of neoliberalism?

AYD: The feminisms with which we identify—antiracist, anti-imperialist, anticapitalist feminisms—are constantly changing. This is something that is sometimes difficult for academics and activists to grasp—that they can't assume that the framework is going to always remain the same. Even those of us who might think that we have attached ourselves to the most generative, the most productive framework have to be careful about allowing that framework to stagnate. Therefore, older generations really have to listen carefully to younger generations. I think that the value of listening is something that we don't place enough emphasis on. Within the abolitionist circles that I operate, I have seen so much change over a relatively short period of time. For instance, we were talking about the role of work around transgender issues. It would have been impossible to imagine twenty years ago.

People like CeCe McDonald,[18] who spent several years in prison and was brutalized and falsely charged with murder when she was defending herself against someone who attacked her. I had the opportunity to spend some time around her at a conference. She's a really amazing activist. Not only around trans issues but around issues of the prison-industrial complex in general. And that conversation has allowed us to rethink the way in which we had imagined the analysis and the struggle against what we call the prison-industrial complex. (This is the value of feminism to me, the flexibility of the frameworks.) To begin to talk about the ways in which the prison institution itself is an apparatus that engages and processes of gendering. That makes it have so much of a broader reach, and it's not only connected to punishment and to prisoners and prisoner's rights and so forth.

Part of the process of working towards the abolition of the prison-industrial complex has to do with the abolition of an ideological apparatus, not only a state repressive apparatus, but it is also about an apparatus that has helped to create and continues to reproduce the whole process of gendering. It is a gendering apparatus, and that would never have become apparent if we had not been willing to embrace the issue of trans prisoner's rights. Feminism allows us to break free of the framework that assumes that what is numerically larger is going to define the issue. So we recognize that even the smallest, most minute issue contains insights that can allow us to move forward in amazing ways. I see feminism as also about methodology, not just about objects of what one is studying or objects of one's organizing but as a method, a methodology, a framework.

LEC: Of how to be in the world.

CTM: Which is why then one can envision futures that are emancipatory or liberatory in the largest possible ways, because it is not about just the concreteness of "we want to live a life that gives us food and shelter" and this and that and the other, which, of course, we all want, but that it allows one to imagine an expansive vision of what it would mean to live in a just world. So what would that mean for you? How would you characterize that?

AYD: I always think that these imaginaries are temporary, because once we have moved to the place we once imagined, we recognize it is so much more complicated. But that's precisely the value of the imagination. What's interesting is that we're often encouraged to think in terms of bodies, and, of course, racism does that, because race is presumed to be attached to bodies, although it is not. We know that. As a matter of fact, that's why when I first read your "Third World Women and the Politics of Feminism,"[19] I found your notion of Third World women as a political project so liberating. I would want to live in a world where the processes of commodification are clearly on their way out of history. What often appear to be very basic wishes are so far out of reach—for example, the very ability to get a free education seems so bizarre today. I would want education to be free from kindergarten or child care all the way up to postgraduate and beyond. That would mean that the very process of education would have to be transformed too. It is not just being able to have free access to what exists now, but that would mean that curriculum would change, structures would change, administration would change, relations would change.

Having spent the majority of my life on college and university campuses, what really continues to bother me is the fact that the workers in these spaces are so invisible even today. Even students or faculty who consider themselves to be most radical don't take into consideration that we have not created a community on these campuses that involves the people that actually enable the work to be done. I always go back to Marx, because Marx decided that the question of leisure time would be solved by reducing the number of hours one works in the day, which somehow or another has got stuck at eight hours. If one looks at the struggles for shorter workdays over the years and centuries, we should definitely be at about three hours a day now. But I imagine people having the opportunity to really follow their passion. Everyone should be able to make art. It doesn't have to be good art, but everyone should be able to express themselves, because I took that really seriously from Marxist analysis—about the fact that we externalize ourselves in the objects that we make and that workers are totally alienated from the products of their labor because of the whole capitalist system. I would want a world in which that was possible. I could go on and talk about any of the basic things and also philosophically about what might it mean to transform human relations and to transform our sense of ourselves.

LEC: Especially in an era when commodification is so intense. Everything that can be commodified is commodified.

AYD: Which is literally everything. Even thoughts.

LEC: Commodified and appropriated, and the state is a master of this now. Even some elements of human relations are commodified, and the state makes it part of its language—from relating to people to telling them how to relate to each other. If you look at the current election campaign, you see some of these ideas are not these peoples'. They come out of elements of struggle that they have appropriated and commodified.

CTM: So what do you see as the future of feminist praxis?

AYD: Yeah, and I think that this might be the time to try to broaden the reach of feminism. I have never been someone who has relied on labels, because even early on my position was that it doesn't really matter whether you call yourself a feminist; what matters most is the work that you do—the activist work, the scholarly work. But I do think that this might be the moment to encourage a more accessible feminism. In November I gave a talk at Vassar to mark the thirtieth anniversary of their women's and gender department. It was called "Our Feminisms." How can we make feminisms accessible to young women and men and to those who don't necessarily directly identify along those binary lines as something that is relevant to their lives? Because it's inevitable that younger generations are going to see feminism as belonging to their mothers or their grandmothers or their great-grandmothers, and not as something that they can take and transform and work with and work on. We're seeing this played out in the elections. So I think this is precisely the period when feminisms can become, and are becoming, more accessible.

I'd like to see young Black men activists, student activists talking about the importance of challenging gender violence. I like the fact that the Black Lives Matter movement has been represented as a movement that is expansive and that addresses queer issues, addresses issues of ableism. For me, feminism is about producing these broad frameworks. It began with a focus on gender, but I think that we know now that the real value of feminism is the ability to create a framework of understanding and analysis that allows us to do what is otherwise impossible, particularly when we rely on these frameworks that assume that there are discrete issues and categories and they don't interact with each other, or at the same time there might be things that need to be pulled apart that we can't. That is what we need today. It appeals to the younger generation in ways that it never appealed to our different generations, because it was not familiar, and it has become more familiar to those who are coming up. It should be more familiar, because they take it for granted and they can move forward with it and create other things that we never could have imagined ourselves.

CTM: So much is about the imagination, right?

LEC: Exactly, but that, too, has been commodified, right? Their notion of feminism, because when you hear "Is this person is feminist?" or "That person is saying that they are feminist," you start thinking through what some of this means.

AYD: I think "Is Beyoncé a feminist?" is a good question because it allows us to engage in conversation. And also there are so many different versions of feminism. There's no way to say yes or no definitively to any question, because there are so many different questions. It's great that these issues are coming up in popular culture. What is progressive at one moment in history is not necessarily progressive fifty years later, or twenty years later. The value of feminism or the value of antiracist, anticapitalist, anti-imperialist feminisms that are Marxist-inflected feminisms is that it allows us to think about the framework of our analysis or of our organizing at the same time that we use that framework to think about whatever it is we are examining. That is a habit that most people have not been able to embrace, because it is a habit that contravenes disciplinary thinking—in disciplinary thinking the framework is what enables everything else, so once you begin challenging the framework, everything falls apart. And feminism allows us to trouble the framework, allows things to fall apart and at the same time put them back together. It allows us to imagine something entirely different.

Further Reflections:
Imagining a Revolutionary Feminist Politics

AYD: The 2016 presidential election has come and gone, and what once might have appeared to be the fictional musings of paranoid pundits has become the political reality redefining the relation of the United States and its leadership to people of this country and the world. Refugees and immigrants from numerous Arab countries are being detained by border officials, and massive demonstrations at international airports are proclaiming militant opposition to the executive order barring people from seven majority-Muslim countries and expressing solidarity with those in detention.

For the last few years, manifest feminist dimensions of the Black Lives Matter movement, including the upsurge in Black student activism, heralded a new era of radical political engagement. The acknowledged leadership of women—including trans women—in these and other movements does not signify a simple substitution of women for men. Rather it announces a critique of past masculinist leadership paradigms anchored in charismatic individualism. The past emphasis on the individual—usually male—leader resulted in a failure to acknowledge both the role of organizers, many of whom have been women, and the agency of the participants in movements for change. As Barbara Ransby demonstrates in her incisive study of Ella Baker's role in the mid-twentieth-century freedom movement,[20] notions of collective leadership that have been taken up by the younger generation are not new. In other words, the younger generation of scholars and activists have already paid close attention to forward-looking yet marginalized insights of the past. Thus the question older scholar-activists should be pursuing is how to contribute a productive intergenerationality to contemporary thought and activism that is based on a willingness of all generations to learn from one another. I like to think of this two-way learning process as "egalitarian intergenerationality."

If public expressions of shock and mourning were the immediate response to the election of Donald Trump, the Women's March, convened the day after the inauguration, heralded a rising collective militancy. This massive gathering of women, men, trans persons, and children on the National Mall in Washington, joined by hundreds of sister marches throughout the country and in other parts of the world, powerfully communicated the message that we intend to resist the many forms of violence encouraged by the current leadership of the United States, whether misogynist, racist, Islamophobic, or xenophobic, and attempts to enforce social and economic exclusion, including attacks on the environment. The potential success of this resistance will certainly depend on the willingness of organizers and participants to insist on the kind of intersectional approach to social justice that has been encouraged by antiracist and anticapitalist feminists over the last two decades. It will depend on the recognition, for example, that water is a feminist issue and that our solidarity with the Standing Rock Sioux as they fight to protect their water (and their land and culture) must also be extended to those who live in Flint, Michigan, as well as in Occupied Palestine, who are also fighting for their water, their lives, and their sovereignty.

As we resist, we must never forget why we are resisting. It is possible to become so ensconced in the process of fighting back that the forces we resist become too central to our understanding of who we are as a community of struggle. We cannot forget that we want to change the world. Thus the call for prison abolition, for example, is not simply a mandate to simply rid the world of prisons, but also a reminder that our worlds will have to be radically transformed and that they will ultimately bear the imprint of the struggles we undertake today.

Photo by Michael Kuttner

Materializing Class, Historicizing Culture

Himani Bannerji

Coming of Age: Himani's Story

Himani Bannerji: I came to Toronto quite grown up at the age of twenty-seven in 1969, in the summertime. I had been teaching at Jadavpur University (Kolkata, India) for five years before then, in comparative literature and English departments. Among other things, my curriculum was teaching new things in literature in the sixties, such as Raymond Williams and Terry Eagleton. There has been a strong communist movement in India—a party, not just a movement, divided between two parties, Communist Party of India (CPI) and Communist Party of India (Marxist) (CPI[M]), the latter came to power in two provinces. We were, as students, influenced by communism. Late in the sixties a new political tendency emerged based on Maoism,[1] also known as the Naxalite movement. The Maoist students occupied both Calcutta and Jadavpur universities, and also the renowned Presidency College. After a long period of occupation, troubles between students and university authorities, and failures of negotiations, the Jadavpur University administration summoned the police, who raided students' residences, including those of women students, which was unheard of, and made many arrests. The vice-chancellor of the university was killed in retribution in broad daylight. There was a massive anti-Maoist upsurge on the part of the state, which eventually led in seventy-four or seventy-five to the period known as the Emergency, imposed by then prime minister Indira Gandhi. The Naxalite movement emerged in the tea gardens of Assam and Bengal and spread through all of West Bengal. In retaliation to student occupations, the provincial police and the army established checkpoints, curfews, and so on, on university campuses. Some places in Bengal became like what I now see in Gaza. The city of Kolkata itself became a war zone. I was a very young faculty member, so you can imagine that there was a lot of excitement and debates and discussion, and then the police coming in and rounding up faculty and students. It was a terrible thing. The city was in a great turmoil and buses were burning. If you left in the evening, you didn't know if you would come back. I grew up through that, and I was between the ages of twenty to twenty-seven.

Though we did not talk generally about women's movement at this point, there was a strong anti-oppression, social justice, economic justice angle to all this. Left political struggles of this time inherited in some way the mantle of anticolonial struggles against British colonialism over the previous hundred years, of fighting against oppression, inequality, and injustice. It became a continuation, if you like, of an incomplete revolution. Or a revolution that didn't happen in India. So China went one way and India went another. Our communist parties became electoral. They gave up extra-parliamentary politics and armed struggle, and India became an aspiring Third World capitalism. That is the background to the problems I'm talking about. The long-awaited independence (1947) had delivered very little for ordinary people, and there was a mass disappointment about it. The present situation in India is now not just disappointing, but grotesque in its failures in its neoliberal phase ideologically compounded with Hindu fundamentalism. The transfer of populations entailed in the Indian independence, as well as loss of property and lives, continued over a period of time. People coming from Bangladesh, or in those days East Pakistan, were not yet settled. You have probably read Mahasweta Devi,[2] Urvashi Butalia,[3] Jasodhara Bagchi,[4] and others, about what happened through all that time.

That was my orientation, but we did read, in the course of all this, material on justice for women, because there was a fair bit of participation of women in Indian independence movements in the different groups, beginning with nationalist armed struggle through the establishment of a "liberated zone" by communists and other participants in Telengana, to the more pacific Gandhian Congress. A vast number of women were present in these struggles. And this is discussed really well by Radha Kumar in her *History of Doing.*[5] It is really a good book, beginning to end. It begins in the nineteenth century and works out this politics first *about* women and then *by* women—beautiful photographs, reproduction of handbills, and so on. It is really worth having. We are the inheritors of that tradition of women's participation in politics.

Mary Wollstonecraft was an important figure in the English department at Jadavpur University.[6] When we were students in the English department, we read eighteenth- and nineteenth-century British women novelists, along with Leninist formulations of "the woman question," because the question of patriarchy was beginning to trouble all the communist/socialist movements at that time. Being part of that ambience, problems of women were not unknown to us. That made me think that it wasn't really a parliamentary question, of representation in the government, but the women's question became a social question—a human question. So that is really my foundation.

At this point of our development we made little connection between our personal and political lives. We knew we had to be ethical, we knew we had to live austerely. We could not expect to live economically rich lives. But we would have to be true to our commitment of social justice and not be exploiters, and we had to dedicatedly work for social betterment and justice. People working in the old Congress and nationalist movements, as well as the communist movements, lived extremely frugal lives. They were people who never had more than a few hundred rupees to live on, if that, and some never married and often lived transient lives in other people's homes. Sacrifice and simplicity were to be the key words in our conduct. We could actually try to live up to that, but we could not yet interpret so well, though we read Wollstonecraft, the connection between personal, family lives and our political commitment. We talked about justice and equality for our mothers and aunts and grandmothers, because we were also a generation that went to schools, universities, and had professions.

The independence really brought a vast number of women to higher education and professional life. Refugee families had to let women and girls work, because now it was no longer possible to keep your daughter at home and get her married. She had to make an earning in order for the family to survive. Ritwik Ghatak in his film, *Cloud Capped Star (Meghe Dhaka Tara)*,[7] is about an amazing young woman who works in offices—supporting her family, her sick father, semiliterate mother, and unemployed brother. The role of girls and women changed in my early growing up quite radically. Suddenly, from one being an object for the marriage market, you knew that you'd have to make a living. Many men and women at that time couldn't marry until advanced age, because they had to raise their younger brothers and sisters. This was a common story then and probably so even now. I think this situation is very familiar to Caribbean and Afro-American families.

Linda E. Carty: Yeah. The oldest daughter—

HB: —is really the head of the family when parents cannot provide anymore. So we got that part about the need for women to work outside of the family, and justice for women and equality in social terms, and wanting to have a space in the educational world, not hang back from arguing and being part of politics, but we didn't think about patriarchal, sexual violence so much in interpersonal relationships and families. We associated it with the communal riots leading up to the partition of India and years following that. Rapes, sexual assault, and mutilation of women's bodies—those were common themes. But family life was left to a large extent unexamined. The interesting thing is that it's not the other part of politics, that in the street, the demonstrations, marches, and other public spaces. It was really learning more about the question of personal relations and how the personal is political. That became a meaningful slogan for me, and I learned it in Toronto. But at the same time, women were learning it in India. Not through me. The influence probably came from feminist efforts of the United Nations, political convergences of women, and various kinds of commissions which were being set up.

At this time two feminist works became extremely important in India: one by Sheila Rowbotham, *Women's Consciousness, Man's World*,[8] and the other by Germaine Greer, *The Female Eunuch*.[9] The latter title and cover, of a woman's torso hanging on a hook, was shocking. It's interesting that people living in different parts of the world who did not know each other touched each others' consciousness. I'm still trying to figure out how that happened, and I have some guesses about that. Around the late sixties and seventies there were a lot of social movements and anti-imperialist movements happening. Somehow, maybe not causally but conjuncturally, there was a connection between these things. Vietnam was my upbringing in terms of feeling politically identified. There was a Bengali slogan which said, "*Amar naam, tomar naam*, Vietnam." *Naam* means "name" in Bengali, so "your name and my name is Vietnam."

These slogans and big marches and bombings and the My Lai massacre happened. On one hand, we were very influenced by the anti-imperialist movements. I remember the plays being done on civil rights movements in the United States when we were in college. There was a very powerful theater director and writer, Utpal Dutt, who was part of the People's Theatre Association, writing plays about the Scottsboro Boys. He did another one on Martin Luther King. The left in general in India got very excited by the Black Panther movement. The news of these events and ideas connected with them were traveling. People knew the name of Angela Davis even when I was in college.[10] That was very important, South Africa was very important, and the Algerian anticolonial revolution, which happened when I was younger, was also very influential. One after the other, colonies were revolting and emerging into independence.

In the seventies and early eighties formal decolonization was accomplished. And Leonard Peltier, of the American Indian Movement (AIM)—which they didn't know much about in India but I knew about here—falsely accused, is still lingering in an American prison to this day. All of this together produced an atmosphere of hopeful struggle everywhere. I remember having discussions about reform and revolution, and [Frantz] Fanon, whom I learned to read here. People were quite scared of him because he so unashamedly talked about armed struggle. In his formulation there is a difference between the two: violence is what the ruling oppressors do; armed struggle is what the resisters do. It would be impossible to make both into the same. What has happened now is that we have forgotten that Fanon talked about armed struggle, reclaiming of land and territories, and anticolonialism, but the fact is that he didn't say go out and just be violent.

Chandra Talpade Mohanty: This is what is happening in Palestine now: that people refuse to actually analyze in that way in terms of resistance.

LEC: Because it's the state that is violent. The state has been perpetrating violence on people every day. But the resistance to the state, those are resistance movements.

HB: The state has the monopoly of violence even in what is claimed to be liberal democracy. Right now what we are watching in the United States is state violence. If people fight back and say there is no other way, they will not acknowledge your resistance as legitimate. People have pleaded and said, "Please," and nothing has worked. People are only human, they have their need for dignity, and [they] rage if they are deprived of that dignity and other necessities of life. How long can people keep on and on in this situation without any negative response? So in the seventies there was an atmosphere—

CTM: A space for certain kinds of revolutionary ideas, which included feminism.

HB: Yeah, which included saying women's lives are human lives, but also English-speaking countries in the West had a more direct feminist movement. When I read Betty Friedan here—*The Feminine Mystique*—it helped me a lot.[11] Because personally I was going through the breakup of a marriage, and through that framework I could better understand what was going on, because it didn't seem like a fight between me and my husband alone, but a kind of a patriarchal frame within which we were both stuck. We parted, but the reason we didn't part very horribly, and remain friends to this day, is that in some way I developed—and he too—a feminist interpretive framework which says that two good people do not necessarily make a good couple, that there is no reason to shame and blame. The situation was helped by lack of property. So what I'm speaking about here is this mixture of the personal and the political life. Politics was personal to me and then personal became political. It wasn't so clear but it was exciting.

There was a group of women with whom I went through many exploratory sessions of consciousness raising, about what I was up to, what they were up to, what sexuality was about, et cetera. We did not learn about those things in our political movements of younger days. We had this church basement where we had meetings for a bit. Then we got one floor of a house and it was called Women's Place. No other public spaces existed for gathering of women. The University of Toronto didn't have women's studies. Forget that—they didn't have Canadian studies, they didn't have Black studies, they didn't have anything of the sort through the seventies. So then I taught my first feminist course in English literature. It was on Sylvia Plath and Anne Sexton and talked about the female body as a metaphor. The male body had been talked about a lot, but no one talked about childbirth, menstruation, and female desire. That was my first feminist course, and it became quite popular. In 1974 I teamed up with a friend of mine, Howard Buchbinder, who had left his US citizenship and migrated here and ran a group called Praxis.[12]

LEC: That was a wave of Vietnam rejecters who came over. Many of us were taught by radical American professors who came here.

HB: People who gave up their American citizenship joined this group called Praxis, and there was also a group called Just Society. Howard and I created a course called "Male-Female Relations," and we co-taught it. We used all the available material. By the time the late seventies came along, there was more and more material. As a literature student, I was absolutely thrilled by reading Kate Millett—*Sexual Politics*.[13] The classics by male English writers suddenly became terribly patriarchal and even misogynist. We knew there was something wrong with them, but we didn't exactly have the words. So it was very good for that. Meanwhile, in the city, groups like the Black Education Project developed.[14] There was the Black Women's Congress, and the Third World Bookstore across from the Bathurst subway station owned by Lennox and Gwen Johnson. They were former communists. And there were also attempts to set up International Women's Day, which was very contentious. We cut our political teeth on various kinds of political dissonances within that process.

In 1973, after the Chilean coup and the killing of [Salvador] Allende, a lot of Chileans came to Toronto as refugees. It was very interesting to see revolutionary Chilean coffee clubs form, where we heard the music of Violeta Para and Victor Jara. Mercedes Sosa also came here. There was a lot of politics in this city. Some of us started writing a little bit of poetry and got ten, fifteen minutes at the end of everything to read our poems. We did a lot of poems at that time, and that's when Dionne Brand started writing, Lillian Allen started writing. I did some, and Krisantha Sri Bhaggiyadatta, Clifton Joseph. Suddenly from nothing there was us. It felt pretty powerful.

LEC: Powerful because it was putting people of color, immigrants' lives in the center. Even though she's right, it might be at the end of the event, but it was there, and then they all started putting out volumes of their poetry, no matter how small.

HB: At that time we had nowhere to publish. Williams-Wallace had a little publishing concern that brought out Dionne's *Primitive Offensive* and *Fore Day Morning*.[15] Krisantha didn't have set hours to work. He had a cleaning company called Domestic Bliss that used to go around cleaning people's kitchens and stoves. Whatever money they garnered, a little bit of that—and we contributed some—came to publishing these books. Lillian Allen's first publication, *Rhythm an' Hard Times*, was through Domestic Bliss,[16] and so was my book of poetry, *A Separate Sky*.[17] Suddenly we were there, so to speak, and it was very good.

LEC: And the works were quite popular among all the communities—activists and scholars.

CTM: There was a sense of camaraderie and collaboration.

HB: The word "Black," as in England, came to stand for resistance politics from the Global South, as we call it now. There was very little competition or going off to major presses and trying to side with them. I remember when at first we began to look at material to teach with, we found very little Canadian material. Fireweed had started towards the mid-seventies, so there was a little bit of material there, but there was really no book, no anthology. In the late seventies a left press here, Between the Lines, asked me to edit a book and I did. They didn't like it. They said that I have to have sixteen-year-olds in my mind's eye and that my writers didn't know how to write. So I went to see Makeda Silvera. Makeda and Stephanie Martin, her partner, had started a little press called Sister Vision.[18] I said to them, "Do you want a selling book?" because once it was out, we could have used it as a textbook. This book had Dionne, Lee Maracle,[19] Roxana Ng,[20]

Sherene Razack,[21] May Yee, Linda [Carty],[22] and my own writing. There were eight or ten essays. Later most of these people became very well known writers.

We thought the people at Between the Lines, the Swift brothers, who researched on oil in Indonesia, were comrades, but they proved not to be. They were trying to tell me that I have to tell these people how to write properly, which I found very offensive. So Makeda said, "Yeah, I want it." Within three or four weeks we put the book out. It was called *Returning the Gaze*.[23] It was snapped up instantly, because it was one collection of local material that we had. We had been relying on the US and UK, and there was good material, but we didn't have relevant Canadian material that addresses sexist-racism or racist-sexism. We had first-wave feminists writing, which are women qua women, but they didn't address particularities created by certain relations existing racist, patriarchal capitalism.

Howard Buchbinder and I started to teach the course "Male-Female Relations" in 1974 for York University, Atkinson College (Continuing Education). (Howard died in 2004.) Still we had no women's studies program, and we didn't have any African American studies or Black studies or antiracist studies, either in York or the University of Toronto. One or two courses were taught at most. I was a part-timer for about eighteen years or so. My daughter was in an MA program before I got a proper job, but I worked a lot as part-time course director. So we taught courses that had feminist and antiracist components, and then I devised a fourth-year course on gender and race for Atkinson. This was a working people's school. Evening classes.

Around 1976 there was a course called "Male and Female in Western Civilization" that was put together by Johanna Stuckey,[24] who was a well-known feminist at York, and several other people brought it together. I was one of the teaching assistants. There was a graduate student called Pat Mills in the Social and Political Thought program at York, who later became a well-known scholar on women, nature, and [Friedrich] Hegel.[25] The course we collectively designed and taught, Pat said, was a long leap from cave to couch, and it was. It began with the Babylonian genesis and it ended with Maya Angelou, with Juliet Mitchell talking about psychoanalysis and women in between. We all attended each other's lectures.

It was nice because we didn't have a hierarchy. It was still like a "women together" and "politics in the university" kind of thing, but unfortunately as we matured and developed as feminist "scholars" and departments were actually starting to be shaped, that disappeared. The university co-opted a lot of this participatory equality. Hierarchies began to appear. Being a woman was superseded by being a faculty member, a part-timer, or a graduate student. I personally feel that we took a lot from everyday lives of ordinary women and we never gave back to the women from whom we took, and that is what intellectuals typically do. In some sense now it has become so academicized that feminist politics in the university is very much institutional politics, and the publications are written in a language that even educated people sometimes can't read. Organizations that had a lot to do with women's groups and so on disappeared. The state started pulling back, and the neoliberalism that we talk [about] showed itself in this move of undoing the managed democracy of the previous period. Defunding of feminist and popular organizations, of course, was central to this problem, but none of the political parties took up, in any real sense, any antiracist feminism. The discourse about women became mainstream and evolved into a talk of the "glass ceiling" and professional advancement.

Trade unions talked a little bit about women's marginalization but actually to this day have not expanded enough to include the new worker, who is transient, precarious, and often a woman. Trade unions remained really strongly tied to formal labor, properly employed labor, when the majority of labor in this country is not that [pro-]labor at all. The face of the worker as projected by trade unions is of a white man, not the face of a Black or "other" worker, nor is it a woman's face. Now I think GM [General Motors] is coming back a bit, but it's changed. The number of people employed is so few, and certainly women are not a part of it.

This is basically what brought me to where I am politically now. Life, really. Politics about women, involving women, and all around women. It became very apparent to many of us that we can't really do politics for social change in any significant way and not involve issues around gender and patriarchy. Now I have been living between two countries for many years and have been able to see similarities and differences between North America and India. My involvement with feminist politics in India also led to working in the establishment of the School of Women's Studies by the late professor Jasodhara Bagchi.[26] She and I were involved in a feminist research project on women's reproductive health and self-perception of health and sexuality. This project was funded by the Canadian International Development Agency (CIDA) and Indo-Shastri Institute (Government of India). We got a lot of money, which we used in order to set up the school, and we bought our computer, our first phones, and other equipment, and Jadavpur University allowed us to house it there. Jasodhara was the director and she marshaled all of us into her service. She had a great ability to bring everybody together. We also had a research project titled "Social Roots of Culture." Many of us worked on the nineteenth century and the rise of the gentlewoman, or the *bhadramahila*. Essays produced from this research became our books eventually: *Inventing Subjects* and *Interrogating Motherhood.*[27] Kavita Panjabi and her contemporaries were still students.[28]

CTM: At Cornell. That's how I knew her.

HB: She was there and then they came back. The School of Women's Studies was a lovely place. We had lots of food and chatted and sat around. It was a great *adda* place to go. That place also has become cold and distant now. There is a lot more money and no *adda* anymore—no hangout, you know. Business is being done.

LEC: Same in the North, same in the South.

HB: Yeah, so it has really become more and more institutionalized, and of course it has gone the direction the university has gone—at York too. Many of us didn't put our teaching in women's studies, because we thought, "Now this lets our home departments off the hook." Students were told, "If you want to do something on women, go to the women's studies." Students said, "We don't want to go to the ghetto; we want to be here and be able to do work on these things here." Sociology was becoming Marx, Weber, Durkheim, the fathers of sociology. The mothers were not at all involved. Anything you wanted to do on gender and patriarchy you could do in development studies as political economy, but all kinds of people working on politics, ideology, development were of the opinion [that] those kinds of things had to go to women's studies. So some of us thought, "We are going to be right here, doing this work in this department, because if we all leave, then we just leave it to them." I think that was a good thing.

Many of my younger colleagues in social sciences do good work, but I think it's become unfashionable to talk about patriarchy anymore, even though patriarchy is more strongly present than ever. Sexual harassment and assault, including rape, in the society at large and in academic institutions, continue to go on, and in fact have increased in the last decade, but it has become unfashionable to talk about grand narratives such as patriarchy or class. It's the ultraliberalism of you-can-be-who-you-want-to-be. I think that edge that was there, something that gave you something to fight about, and with, has yielded to ultraliberalism, which, in the name of flexibility, has actually depoliticized and made it difficult to make a judgment about what is right and what is wrong. It's not right to be making a judgment; no one can, because the one thing that they are certain about is that everything is uncertain. Yes, I'm talking about postmodernism.

LEC: Some of that has to do with the fact that the state has an agenda so many have given in to. Look at what the state's role has been in regularization of certain kinds of discourses, thinking, even inside the academy. You find scholars withdrawing and retreating, making the decision not to teach these things, but some of us still do that kind of work. We're still teaching it. Initially it seems foreign to students, and then pretty soon they understand, because you really tie it to their lived realities, so they can see how they are being oppressed. I think when we fail to do that, we are no longer good feminists. It has to be acknowledged that to give in to the state's agenda like that is like being complicit in your own subordination.

CTM: Yes. Himani, if you were to think about what it is that we need within the feminist, antiracist, Marxist social movements that we care about right now, which are also what seem to be the movements that will make it possible for us to imagine what it means to not be complicit in the neoliberal agenda, what do we need to do to create solidarities and connections across the divides that are in place at the moment? As you say, the neoliberal narrative of everything is uncertain, so we can't even make certain kinds of judgments, which we have in common, actually; that if we were to hear each other speak, we would know we are making the same analysis and judgments, and therefore we would have things that we can fight about and fight with.

LEC: What brought activists and scholars to the point of deciding they're not going to do this kind of work? Nobody held a gun to their heads. They have given into a neoliberal agenda that says Marxism is not cool anymore. It's not even not cool; it's not relevant.

CTM: So patriarchy is not fashionable and Marxism is not relevant.

LEC: That's really the crux of the question. What needs to happen to turn those things around?

HB: Well, none of us have any crystal ball. None of us can come up with a really definitive solution. You're right; no one took a gun to our heads and said, "Do this." That's where we have to realize that it's not causality; it's environmental—the development of an environment of anti–social justice projects that basically perverted demand for social justice into contained and managed administrative ruling relations. That is a problem, because we wanted everything and we got this perverted little contained space within which to do our little things.

We wanted a holistic politics, and we got a little stall in the vending booths of the academic world, and this is our little stall where our books are being sold and we also have our place. In the beginning we might have thought that it is too tight or too totalistic to want something so big; we need to include more and more. The more we included, the more we got excluded until some of us became quite marginal in our own political world. It is not causal but a few things that came into a constellation together.

It happened around the nineties, particularly the mid-nineties on. Though we never really relied on the Soviet Union, the defeat of the Soviet Union—essentially the disappearance of an empire, if you like—also gave a very triumphalist rhetoric to capitalism. The best we could get was liberalism, and that seemed to be the open thing. It was the end of ideology, it was the end of history, it was socialism on the trash cans or trash heaps. So all these kinds of things became very important to discourage people for a while. Not that the Soviet Union was our model. Certainly not mine, nor that of anybody coming from Third World politics. For example, CPI(M) had nothing to do with Moscow. If anybody disappointed us, it was China, by turning towards a neoliberal communism, which killed the communism in West Bengal. After thirty-three years, we lost in the election over land that the government was taking to give away to the industries practically for free. So we got disappointed, and that was part of the triumphalist moment.

Something happened and I am not quite sure how to trace its trajectory, but I was trying to write an article on ideology—the history of it, pure and simple, in a dictionary kind of way. I found that almost all writing on ideology disappeared, even if it was a wooden "ruling ideas of any age or ideas of the ruling class" kind of slogan. In its place came something called cultural studies, and the turn was made from [Antonio] Gramsci's notion of hegemony, which was totally appropriated without looking at the moment of contradictions and force, to simply some kind of administered ideological device. One of the books I saw in that time was the book by Laclau and Mouffe on socialist strategy.[29] I noticed that class struggle, understood in a very wide sense, was excluded, and social movement went this way while class movement went that way. Now, if we could bring them back together and open up the boundaries of class—my own political and conceptual dilemma of *Can you do the experience of being a woman and also do class?* Obviously, we had to socialize the concept of class, but we all also have to materialize it and historicize the concept of culture. This is easier said than done. Anyone can say it right now: "Here I am." But how do you do it? How do you create social movements that have a double edge like that, which don't have to do everything at once but orient it in a different way? Suddenly all writing on ideology and politics ceased and culture became an alibi for becoming nonpolitical, and what was once missing in the economism now has become culturalism.

As teachers we have access to young minds in a way that other people don't. Every year a lot of people go through our hands—more than a political party's hands. Relating the experience of my students to what they know with what we are teaching is key. I taught a course in development studies in the summer. The women taking degrees in the summer—bus drivers and [the supermarket] Loblaws workers—they knew right away how capitalism works. They knew primitive accumulation back to front, because their families had to be turfed out of Jamaica, and land was completely taken away. I didn't have to tell students that US corporations destroyed the dairy industry in Jamaica. One student told me she saw milk going down the drain. She was coming back from school, and she saw milk in the drain and told her mother, and her mother and everybody came to see milk in the drain, and they couldn't even rescue the milk, because it was mixed in the drain. Then I showed them the film called *Life and Debt.*[30]

LEC: This is the key. We have to tie people's lived realities and experiences to these theories so they can understand that they made them. That's where academics are failing.

HB: Yeah, because they really don't have any social relationship with the people of that class and background. They don't hang out with them; they don't really care what people living in high-rise slum suburbs here are going through. They don't know people like that. Many of my colleagues wear designer clothes, even if they buy them from Winners [an off-price department store chain]. The clothes that people wear now to teach are corporate power clothes.

LEC: Yet they do not see a connection between that and what they are teaching, nor do they see the separation between them and the class of the people they are teaching.

HB: They do not. I had a class full of very young people who had children, and they said, "We were bad when we were little." Got pregnant at fifteen years, a couple of kids, living with mother. They are working in three jobs. They are Loblaws workers and so on and looking after children and going to school. It was really stunning.

Further Reflections:
Imagining a Revolutionary Feminist Politics

HB: When we hear the word "fascism" we can think of a situation where the workings of political democracy are absent, and we associate this phenomenon with pre–Second World War European developments. The fascism of our time cannot be an exact replay of that. Since experiments and experiences of capitalist states have allowed for refinement of the ruling apparatus, a country such as the United States has developed and can continue to sharpen a rule of total control through various executive orders, electronic and other modes of surveillance, and using the alibi of national security and economic needs to create a state that is fascistic in potential.

Those who oppose Donald Trump's vision of the United States and his methods for "making America great again" obviously realize this. They also see that Trump's projected new normal has been built on decades of development of neoliberalism in the United States itself. Thus activism and critical expositions and historical social research conducted through the critical perspective of feminist antiracism and anti-corporatism have constantly brought our attention to developments that have culminated in Trump's worldview and reworkings of the political apparatus. Movements such as Occupy, Black Lives Matter, or those culminating in the Standing Rock resistance, and critical condemnations of the US prisons, immigration policies, and dire situation of unemployment, are all there for us to draw from. The ideological aspects that naturally accompany an economy in crisis, which is produced by neoliberalism with its inherent contradictions, have been manifest in the aggressive sexism bordering on misogyny and white supremacism accompanied with Islamophobia.

In my view, no socially or politically conscious person—no one even vaguely concerned with social justice—can avert their eye from these realities. Our everyday lives in all their essential features are encroached upon by these growing tentacles of fascism. By whatever name we wish to call it, we have to work on the side of socialism, which democratizes popular entitlement, participation, and development of human capacities. The time has come to remind ourselves of the famous choice indicated by Rosa Luxemburg between socialism and barbarism.[31] To this end we have to make a distinction between true popular movements, which attend to the economic and emotional well-being of people, which simultaneously nurture the material and the spiritual (spiritual as opposed to institutional religion), and the brand of populism devoid of any real social empowerment and resource entitlement offered by Donald Trump in his worldview based on the need for an enemy, on hatred of the "other." This kind of populism, which strives for a hierarchical citizenship and mono-ethnicity trumped up on white supremacy, is what we would see as staples of fascism.

But we cannot only point the finger at the United States. Capital in its neoliberal phase has created a particularly crisis-ridden toxic environment all over the so-called developed parts of the West, which has been further complicated by their dangerous imperialist military incursions in the Middle East, and the indescribable destruction visited upon countries in the region has catapulted towards power far-right political parties in Europe. The countless number of political refugees who are trying to find safety in Europe, which has precipitated death and displacement in their lives, are finding the doors being shut. White supremacism and Islamophobia also provide the core of the vision for new Europe. The presence of fascist political leaders such as Marine Le Pen or leaders in Austria, Hungary, or Alternative for Germany, among others, have not hesitated to evoke their Nazi past as a positive option, while Brexit has also projected the same mentality. The immigration policies of all Western countries have displayed a basic distortion of liberal democracy. Race and gender are intrinsic components of these antidemocratic measures, making bodies of Muslim women pawns in their power politics. The colonial discourse of orientalism, itself a form of racism, has created the idea of an enemy within.

While this state of affairs endangers the lives of all non-European peoples living in Europe and the US, Canada, Australia, et cetera, it has fundamentally sought to alter the political map of the Western world. The legislated proscription of *burqa*, *burqini*, or *niqab* is not only an action aimed at controlling Muslims, but it also signals the aspirations and the ability to control the lives of all people living within the country. This brings us to the adage of Pastor [Martin] Niemöller with reference to the Nazis, in which he showed that once the state's authoritarian impulse becomes a totalist one, not just Jews and communists but everyone else is stuck in a crisis.

In conclusion, I would like to say that all aspects of democracy that seem to have become fragile these days must be treasured and fought for. Connections between social movements ranging over large fields must be mapped up, and solidarity among struggles is critical. Capital's expansion into a total socioeconomic and political form requires an equally total network of resistance. It is in this process that we will be able to resolve the relations between race, gender, and class in a political and imaginative manner.

Photo by Leslie Feinberg

Being in Motion

Building Movements across Generations

Minnie Bruce Pratt

Coming of Age: Minnie Bruce's Story

Minnie Bruce Pratt: I do have a story about my first political action, but I will preface it by saying that the meaning of this story is what you gain for yourself if you stick to your principles that seem to be about other people. I was asked to do a keynote for Creating Change,[1] an LGBT organizational developmental conference, in the nineties. It was supposed to be about dealing with racism, because this was when Creating Change wasn't as thoroughly and programmatically committed to dealing with issues of racism and multinationality as they are now.

So they had me come and talk, and I decided that I did not want to do that alone as a white woman. I thought it would be more productive if I did it with an African American lesbian, and so I told them that I would not do it by myself. I wanted to have a dialogue with someone, and I said I thought Jewelle Gomez would be a good person.[2] So we set that up, and Jewelle and I started writing back and forth to develop a set of questions we would ask each other. I had questions I would ask her, she had questions she would ask me, and we decided we would both dwindle the list down and we would both answer each question.

One of the questions she came up with was "What was your first political act?" I had never thought about that searchingly. What I recovered from my memory of my life is this: In the fall of 1966 I was eligible to vote for the first time. I turned twenty in September and the elections were in November. This was in Alabama. I was at the University of Alabama, where I became an undergraduate a year after George Wallace stood in the schoolhouse door, as it's called.[3] The "schoolhouse door" was Foster Auditorium, which was where you went to register for classes. And that's the door he stood in. The National Guard federalized and met him, along with the deputy US attorney general and African American people registering in Foster Auditorium.

At twenty I was still an undergraduate there, and the civil rights movement had been going on for many years, and I had been seeing those actions on the TV. I saw the black-and-white footage from the assaults on the Children's March in Birmingham.[4] I saw black-and-white footage of the Freedom Riders coming off the burned bus in Anniston [Alabama], the freedom fighters beaten up. There was a lot of coverage. The audio to the visuals (the announcers) was all white supremacy, because the media was owned by business interests committed to white supremacy. And everyone I heard in authority was a white supremacist: my minister, my preacher, all the preachers in my town, the mayor of the town, the editor of the newspaper, and my parents. All of my teachers and all of my professors were silent, so I didn't know where they stood, but they were not opposing it.

I had never heard a person raise their voice and verbalize opposition except what I saw on that footage. I knew it was wrong what was happening, but I didn't have any language, or argumentation, or much knowledge to articulate that. I didn't have a real political or ethical position; it was just a feeling in response to what I saw happening to the people that I saw laying down their lives to oppose it. Sometimes, of course, their voices were allowed in but not all that very often.

So at twenty years old I went to vote in my first election. That was the year that the Lowndes County Freedom Democratic Party was formed, in Lowndes County, with farmers whose political experience dated all the way back to organizing in the thirties and forties with the Communist Party, and with the Sharecroppers Union, and at that time with SNCC,[5] also in Lowndes County. They organized a separate Democratic Party, because, of course, the white Democratic Party was completely segregationist. That organizing also happened at the state level in Mississippi as well. I didn't know anything about all of that. I went to vote in the second floor of our courthouse, which was named for my grandfather because he was the probate judge for fifty years in our county.

On the second floor was a big open room. There were no voting booths. There was no privacy in voting. Voters just got their ballot and sat down at a table and marked the ballot. This is what I remember about my ballot. There were candidates that were marked with the rooster. That was the emblem of the segregationist Southern Democratic Party. There were other candidates that were marked with a Black Panther [logo], because the Alabama Freedom Democratic Party had put up candidates. I don't remember if that was just for my county or for the state. I don't remember anything except there was the Black Panther, and I don't remember if I had ever seen the Black Panther before. I don't think it was being shown on the TV, but I knew what it was. I knew it was the symbol of the people that were laying down their lives and bodies. I picked up my pencil and I started to mark my vote by the Black Panther. My father had come with me to vote. He came and stood over me and said, "You can't do that," and I said, "Yes, I can," and I marked my mark. I put it in the voting box, and I left. I'm sure they went immediately or at the end of the day and tore it up, but it didn't matter. That was my first political act. I only recovered that memory because

I had demanded that I co-dialogue with an African American lesbian, and Jewelle asked me. It was a lesson for me to remember.

Linda E. Carty: So with that great opening and wonderful memory, and reflecting on the last four decades of your life work as a feminist, how would say that your work has impacted the lives of women?

MBP: I should speak to how I hope [it has], because it's always very difficult to know what an impact one has had. I am about to be sixty-nine, so four decades takes me back to twenty-nine. I became actively political in my late twenties. I do know that the writing that I have done on being an antiracist white woman has made a difference, and the essay in *Yours in Struggle*, "Identity: Skin, Blood, Heart,"[6] was used not just academically but in organizing groups. It has been circulated in ways I don't even know about. I believe it was effective because it emerged at a particular moment in the organizing wave of second-wave feminism. I would preface saying that it had an effect by saying that my ability to write that essay came, not unlike the anecdote about Jewelle and me having a conversation, because women of color within feminism or women's liberation were organizing, writing, producing texts, creating organizations, pushing white women to be accountable around racism not just in their personal life but in organizational ways and so forth. So that essay came after a lot of work had already happened.

In the essay I reference people and texts, specifically by women of color whose work had impacted me. There is a rolling, wavelike effect upon which the essay goes, in part because Chandra and Biddy wrote about it.[7] It gets picked up programmatically through your work, and people started using it in classes. So that antiracist work has had an impact only in conjuncture with the larger framework of organizing. I couldn't have written it without previous work. Even if I had written it in relation to that previous work, it still would not have had the impact that it had if there had not been an ongoing organizing and consciousness raising around racism. I do not want to overestimate the work that the essay did. I think how maybe it is not used as much now, but it is still in use. I think about how awful it is that it is still needed. I'm glad that it is still useful, and I also wish that it were not still useful. I wish that it had fulfilled its historic task and then we were able to go on to other tasks.

Chandra Talpade Mohanty: This is how I think about "Under Western Eyes."[8] Exactly the same way, written in the mid-eighties, and I wish it was not needed, but it feels as relevant now as it was twenty years ago.

MBP: I look at the dynamic, incredible, and central organizing that is being done now under the banner of Black Lives Matter, and I think, "Well, there we are." Within that context, I do feel like the essay still has something to offer, even now, even as other issues are brought forward. I do think that is another contribution that I have made. As I have been able to move into understanding historical materialism, Marxism, and dialectical materialism, and as I have studied, educated myself, and found my own comrades, I have worked to integrate that analysis with the antiracist work that I have done. Some of that writing has been for *Workers World* newspaper.[9] I wrote some long essays that are only available digitally. I wrote a long piece on Reconstruction in the South, talking about the material basis for the unfinished revolution there and the overturning of that. I wrote a more personal, creative nonfiction piece called "When I Say 'Steal,' Who Do You Think Of?,"[10] based on a conversation I had with one of my cousins in Alabama about stealing—who steals and who doesn't. He is a white working-class guy. When I say to him things like "We take the profit motive out, then a lot of what you want would be possible," he completely gets that, but there is this other part of him that is so imbued with racism.

It was an interesting conversation, because I saw on one level how superficial his resistance to truly radical ideas was, and on the other hand the depth of the racism with which the owning classes have imbued the white working class and what a deep struggle that is. I think that is absolutely winnable, but it has to be waged staunchly. That is my trajectory. I am not talking about feminism, but of course I see this as completely part of my fabric as someone who is part of women's liberation. Because how can we change any of what happens to us as women if we do not also engage with these other oppressions? I saw that early on as an impossibility. My life as a white woman would never be different if I did not oppose racism and did not oppose class oppression, because I was trained by my parents to identify with the white owning class as a woman and to perpetuate those values.

CTM: A lot of people have talked about the fact that when you occupy certain marginalized positions, then you are able to see the power structure in certain ways and make certain broad-based connections among and between movements, issues, and identities so that you can understand how connected all of these struggles are.

MBP: How I understood all of this at the very beginning was that I began to live as a lesbian and was punished for it. My place as a white woman was shaken. My relative privilege as a white woman suddenly just shattered because I began to live as a lesbian. I lost custody of my children. After getting divorced from my husband, I tried to rent an apartment, but I could not rent an apartment as a divorced woman in Fayetteville, North Carolina. I could not get anybody to rent to me. I stepped outside what I was allowed as a white woman, and that was it. I explore in the essay what happens when you step outside that circle of protection, not understanding that you have been protected, not understanding what that privilege has been. That could happen at any time for any woman, but whether or not one can build on the understanding that comes from being punished for stepping outside depends on what movement is in motion at the time and what kinds of understandings that movement can offer about women and women's oppression.

Right now there are a lot of women who are being punished and suffering for asserting their autonomy in different ways—sexually, in their work lives—but the women's liberation movement is not visible to them, so they cannot access from that movement, as I did, an analysis of what is happening to them. I had access to the women's liberation movement, and I knew what was happening to me as soon as it started happening to me, because I was part of women's liberation, tangentially. I had access to some of the texts, and I certainly had access to the women who were in motion. I heard them, I listened to them, and I knew immediately. I knew it was not me who was to blame. I knew I was being punished. I knew that patriarchal law and class law were being invoked, and then out of that came the connections you are referring to. Not just because as a white woman I understood but because as a lesbian who was a white woman, I stepped outside those boundaries, and I had a movement that gave me the analysis to understand what was happening.

LEC: That was a very interesting history that you gave us. The backdrop is so powerful because it's a very different history from most white feminist histories.

CTM: Or what we now see as white feminist history.

LEC: Because it comes from a space of having always had a conscientization of race, having always worked with women of color; being in the South, and looking around you and seeing racism informed your consciousness very differently.

MBP: That is so important. Consciousness rises out of material circumstances. I say the movements saved me. They gave me a life, those movements. Then the question for now is, What is in motion now?

CTM: Exactly. If feminism now is about "lean in," what kind of conscientization is that going to bring? This brings me to our next question. Your history and your genealogy in some ways is very generational, because it is about the movements that were on the ground, that were so much a part of your own conscientization. Move to now, 2015, and think about what are the challenges that are coming up for feminists now across countries, sexualities, race, et cetera. In thinking about building complex analyses and explanations for what is happening in the world, and therefore the multiple struggles that we have to engage in, what are the challenges if conscientization is not happening in the same way, because the movements on the ground are not the same movements anymore? In fact we have a very neoliberal world, where certain inequities are perhaps more visible now than they were before, and where forms of resistance are appropriated, immediately consumed, mobilized, depoliticized, and domesticated. So what are the challenges?

LEC: And they make the material conditions seem different.

MBP: I see things a little differently than that question points, because what I am seeing—here, on the [Syracuse University] campus, and not just here but nationally—is how the neoliberal glaze is shattering for people on the ground. Regular working people—the so-called low-wage movement, which is not just people of color but certainly the organizing is led by women of color—all over the world are participating in massive organizing going on around the crushing weight that is on people because of profit making. The reports that I see coming in from all over the US are about solidarity. Not easily won solidarity, but growing solidarity and a kind of dropping of illusions—the illusions around capitalist democracy, what it is going to give people, and then an opening to ask "If that's not working, then what?" I see a lot of questions and desire to talk about other possibilities. I see it in THE General Body organizing here on campus, which has been making an attempt to cross boundaries, to build not a theoretical unity, but an on-the-ground [unity].[11] The state is taking away things that people need, or they are not supplying things that people need. Here the administration is taking away programs that would support lower-income people and people of color; they're not supplying needs for people with disabilities. So what happens when all of the people who are affected by that come together and try to present a united front to push it back? Which they did, they pushed it back. Not complete wins, but they pushed it back. THE General Body just got through pushing it back again around trying to cut the health benefits.

What I am seeing is the material conditions—the austerity—that the public relations of capitalism try to make disappear, but the people who are living it know it has not disappeared. They are living it. In fact, it is getting worse. It is not improving, even though the media machine is trying to convince people that it is improving. The figures just came out about how many cities there are where if people lose their jobs, they cannot last longer than three months without selling something—that is, people who have something to sell. In Buffalo, New York, seventy-five percent of the people cannot survive. In Birmingham, Alabama, sixty-five percent of the people cannot survive. What happens when those people start getting together to push back? That's Black Lives Matter.

You are seeing a direct response to state violence, which is about enforcing austerity. There's a pushing back there. There are people who are saying they are against the state repressing people and harming people. The very concrete manifestation of that are huge demonstrations. The state is oppressing and harming people. I am seeing the hashtags "Black Lives Matter in education," "Black Lives Matter in health care," and then it extends and extends. Just the fact that the state in Ferguson, Missouri, felt that it could target people of African descent and get away with it was the spark, but the potential for people coming together is immense. We are seeing it around the world—Greece, Spain, India.

Obviously the crisis is about "So how do people bridge those differences to be organizationally together?" but that has to be worked out on the ground. It is not something we can sit here and say, "It should happen this way" or "It should happen that way." To me the challenge is more organizational. How does one build, from the ground up, and across that generational gap of people who have been through this struggle before? How does one build those connections to put together some structures that can endure through the kinds of changes that are necessary for people to affirm each other and still stay together in the struggle? Those structures are going to go through many permutations. We have no idea what they might be. They have to be built by the people that are in motion together with the people who have been in motion, but not just theoretically. It's going to look different in different regions. The people in Tennessee who are dealing with things in Tennessee are going be struggling with different things than, say, the people in California, but then how do those connections get put together? People are trying different things. There is the People's Power Assemblies in Baltimore, Philadelphia, and Wisconsin.[12]

I don't know the answer to these questions. Only as people come together do the structures emerge. I have been reading [Leon] Trotsky's *History of the Russian Revolution*. I have a mentor, Milt Neidenberg, who was a union organizer in Bethlehem Steel in Buffalo, who is in his nineties. I told him with great enthusiasm I am reading Trotsky's *History of the Russian Revolution*. I was all excited about the details—for example, how did they do it? Milt said to me, rather sternly, "That was Russia in 1917 and 1918, and this is the United States. Let's talk about what you are going to read next." I go, "Okay, right, right." So they had the soviets, but that came out of a particular material set of circumstances, and we are in a different set of circumstances, where heavy industry is pretty much gone, until it starts coming back because the dollar favors it, but right now we are talking about service workers, teachers, and a different set of organizational demands.

CTM: Also, in terms of women's movements, or feminist's movements, we are talking about incredible exacerbations of violence against women, around the world, which is part of the shift in material circumstances, the rising violence of the state, of militarization, and occupation.

MBP: Yes, and I see emerging out of the new wave of labor organizing or worker center organizing where those concerns that used to be allotted to feminism or women's issues are now being moved into class-based organizing. For example, when the Women's Fightback Network in New York puts out their list of demands, every issue is a working woman's issue.[13] That means violence against women in the workplace—rape, beating, sexual harassment—and it means wages that cannot support the women who have a family to support.

LEC: You have done some great looking back. Now we want you to imagine what kind of world you would like to see for women of tomorrow, as a wonderful anticapitalist, as a poet, as a feminist, and as somebody who has been in the struggle for so long. What does that imagination look like?

MBP: Before I talk about the future, I will say something about the imagination. I am a poet,[14] so I have had to think a lot about the imagination. One of the things I understood as I was doing anti-racist work was how profoundly my imagination had been distorted by white supremacy. Of course, Toni Morrison has written about the imagination and about language; for example, what does it mean to be a writer when the imagination—your tool—is contaminated? Polluted. Your tool is damaged by racism. That certainly was true of my imagination—my language, my vocabulary, my images, my metaphors, my idea of what human beings were. So for me, antiracist work has been organizing and also being demanding of myself in relation to my writing that I not replicate white supremacy in how I do my work. The only way that has changed, as I said earlier, is in collective work, in actual on-the-ground work, with people of color, women of color, antiracist white people, people who are opposed to capitalism, opposed to profiting off of other people's labor and bodies.

As I went through that process, my ability to imagine differently was changed, and other possibilities opened up to me. Even with all of that, I could not have imagined, by myself, for instance, being able to get married to Leslie.[15] I did not imagine that that would happen in my lifetime. It was not individual imagination that made it happen. It was collective imagination, collective hope, and also the springing from moment to moment of collective work together, so that with each step and each spring forward, another possibility opened up.

It is hard to answer your question, because I know from my own experience how limited the individual imagination is. What I hope for in the future, and what I believe based on dialectical materialism, is possible not because we think about it, but because we look at what *is*, and we try to intervene, with others, into what is. If we were able collectively to make those interventions, what I would hope for would be an end to capitalism, an end to people profiting on the bodies and work of other people. That's a collective imaginary. We are only going to get there together. By "us" I don't mean the one percent; I mean the "us" who do the work of the world. An end to profiting off the labor of women's bodies, of the labor of men, too, of children, of people of all nationalities, and the hope that, as that struggle is waged over time, the imagination of a full life could be bread and roses too.

I think about it when I teach, because my training as a teacher came not from the academy but from the movement; doing writing workshops with my peers; my peers teaching me how to teach. I know that the ability to write wonderful poetry is in everybody if they are given room, encouragement, and access to their own life experience without being told it is meaningless, being told instead that it is meaningful. Even inside this university, as repressive as the structure is, I see that in my classroom if a space is made and collective affirmation is offered, people can do brilliant work. I think about what the world would be like if everybody had a chance to do their own work, whatever their own inclination and their own skills and temperament might lead them toward. What the world could be without our being limited by a system that tells us to prey on each other, and that the only way that people can excel is through this system that tells us that we have to stand on other people to excel. I know that is a big lie, because I have seen even in these limited ways what incredible brilliant work people can make together. That is my hope.

CTM: Some of this imagination has to do with finding a way to construct relationships in a way on different grounds with each other too.

MBP: I see it as only happening in the struggle; it's the place I've seen it happen. Or people who are in the struggle and who take that into some other area of their life that is not liberated territory yet. So it is not really about constructing new relationships; it is about being in the struggle and the relationships that are made out of that. Of course, that is a very difficult, messy, complicated process, but also it is where life is.

LEC: It also has to be work of intent. One has to be conscious enough to work on intent.

MBP: The real struggle is to be conscious while we are doing it. The real struggle is for consciousness, but as that is given to us out of the material moment—how to claim it and hold on to it with each other.

CTM: I think about the title of the book we didn't do: "At Home in the Struggle."

MBP: Although now I wouldn't use that.

CTM: What would you call it?

MBP: The reason why I wouldn't necessarily call it that is . . . because of some of the work I am doing, more and more about home and family, and about how the family that is in the home is still a mechanism of the state. Even the enlarged definition of family that is being allowed now in terms of LGBTQ people is just bringing it into a family that is still a mechanism of the state. That means that that place is problematic to me in a way that it always has been problematic since I came to consciousness. Now I think that a new kind of family is only going to come about as part of an anticapitalist struggle, and that only then will it really, truly be "love makes a family," "family is by choice," because everything that is weighted down on the family now, that is forced upon the family's survival as the buffer against utter destitution, that would be lifted from the family. It would be a whole different life for women.

Further Reflections:
Imagining a Revolutionary Feminist Politics

MBP: Repression and struggle are both accelerating at a rapid pace in this era of dead-end capitalism. The aim of the owners of the world is to divide us—the "workers and oppressed peoples of the world"—from each other. We are many, and they are few. Only by dividing us and channeling us into the old mechanisms of power for profit can we be kept from asserting our power for liberation. So solidarity must be our aim, above all. To forge a fighting movement independent of both and all parties of capital. To forge that movement at a wide and at a local, daily level—listening with patience, learning from each other, struggling with each other, and pressing onward always.

Perhaps this call sounds familiar; perhaps it sounds obvious. And words will not make it come into being. We are fighting against the material reality wrought by the cruel hand of racism, woman-hating, queer-phobia, disability-despisal, Islamophobia, all the hatreds fomented and carried out by the powers that be. This era calls upon us to denounce those hatreds, to defy state power and to defend ourselves against yet unknown assault and repression. Only coordinated solidarity will enable us to defend ourselves. How we do this may range from mass demonstrations that are a constant indication of the material relation of forces to local self-defense and rapid-response teams with which we will do our best to keep our friends, neighbors, comrades from being carried away from us, from being locked away, from being attacked and exploited by a capitalism frenzied for profit.

Solidarity will not be forged with words. Solidarity will be forged in on-the-ground struggle to liberate our lives, our bodies, our minds, our imaginations, our daily routine, and our futures.

If We Jump Up

Let new words leap out of our mouths.
Let our hands be astonished at what we have made, and glad.
Let us follow ourselves into a present not ruled by the past.
If we jump up now, our far will be near.

—Minnie Bruce Pratt, *Inside the Money Machine*

Photo by Jerry Riley

Bridging through Time

*Inhabiting the Interstices
of Institutions and Power*

Amina Mama

Coming of Age: Amina's Story

Amina Mama: I can trace my awareness of gender differences all the way back to my childhood in the north of Nigeria, growing up and being in schools there. I went to a mixed primary school and then a high school, formerly a convent, which had girls from all over the country, Muslim and Christian, and many languages. Some of the women I was at school with left to get married young, without completing education. I came from a liberal, mixed-race family, so it was clear my path was going to be different. When you live in any Third World context, if you are observant you see there are very sharp contradictions all around you. On the one hand, there are people living extremely affluent lives, and on the other, you are surrounded by evidence of poverty. I used to find that harshness disturbing as a child. I think that is probably where my awareness of social contradictions began, especially seeing what was happening to women, always working, always struggling, always surrounded by children.

There is one well-known story that had a profound effect on me, from the late seventies. It is the story of a young woman, Hauwa Abubakar, who was given in marriage to a much older man and ran away from her new marriage. Her family returned her and she ran away again, and they returned her, and she ran away the third time, and her family took her back to the husband, who then beat her so badly she had to have her legs amputated, and a little later, she died. I heard about it because Women in Nigeria,[1] which was at that time proud to be a socialist feminist organization with chapters across Nigeria, took up the case. One of the things that came to attention was that the reason her family had to keep sending her back was because they were indebted to the husband, who was their landlord. In Hauwa's story you can immediately see the linkage between gender and class. That has stayed with me.

Chandra Talpade Mohanty: When was that?

AM: This was in the early eighties, I think. I remember that as a critical moment, being at home in Nigeria, and becoming very aware of how class and gender worked together. But I think many things inform my thinking.

The civil war broke out twenty years before the Hauwa Abubakar incident—when I was ten years old. My recall is that it started in Kaduna, the town where we lived, with the assassination of the Sardauna of Sokoto, and the anti-Ibo pogrom—the things that Chimamanda has written about, almost half a century later. We witnessed people fleeing en masse from state violence, from mob violence, and having the neighborhoods where we lived raided by gangs who were searching out and slaughtering people. We hid one of our playmates under my bed while this was going on, and I recall my father persuading masked men at the door that we had no one for them! In the morning we took him to the station to take a train back to the east. At that time I did not think about gender, but one memory I have is of the women with children and loads at the station, and men sweating and pushing everyone about. My mother was giving the women tins of milk and things to get on these trains that would take them back to the east. At that time, for us in the north, the war was more fear and games than actual violence. Even then it was obvious from that while the men went away to fight, the situation was bad for poor women and children. Without knowing it, people talked in hushed tones about "the Igbos" and "Northerners," and it is with hindsight I can see that the war was talked about in ethnic language, and that somewhere in all that, Christians had cause to fear Muslims. That is [my] childhood memory of historic events. I think that if you witness that kind of thing and sense that there is something significant in it, then you naturally develop a lot of questions that stay with you—about how society is arranged, how it is divided, and what happens to different groups of people in those fairly extreme contexts.

The second thing that kept me thinking and developing radical ideas was in the UK. I was a member of the early Black women's movement in South London. By this time I was studying and getting involved in antiracist struggles. The early eighties was a time of a lot of inner-city violence in London 1981, the so-called Brixton riots, which we all called the "uprisings." My sense of connection there saw me getting involved me in community-level politics through the Brixton Black Women's Group (BWG),[2] which at that time was very political. I followed up with my earlier off-the-syllabus reading in the BWG study group: Lenin, Marx, Mao. I learned about Claudia Jones for the first time,[3] because there used to be a large portrait of her on the wall of the Black Women's Center in Stockwell.

I became very aware of what was going on in the UK prisons, how Black people were being rounded up and how the court process sent them to jail. We saw how the same policeman would lie under oath to testify against people arrested at five different locations. It was set up like that. It was shattering at the time, but I learned about how the "British bobby" actually manifested in Black communities: en masse, heavily armed up, wielding extra-long truncheons.

I mention these two examples—one from home in Kaduna, and one from inner-city London—because many years later my interest in antiviolence work and resisting militarization has persisted. I spent my early life moved back and forth between these locations— Kaduna and London.

I also had the travel bug, so as a student, the affordable means was hitchhiking. I was able to get around to a number of places where revolutionary things were happening. So, for example, I went overland across Turkey and Iran to Afghanistan in seventy-eight. Afghanistan had just ousted the monarchy and was having something of a socialist revolution. Because at that time it was the Cold War, the Russians had at that time invited in as advisers. But at the same time, all the *mujahideen* were being supported by the West, to serve as a " bulwark against communism." I saw Afghan women at that time in the short revolutionary moment wearing skirts or jeans, working in banks, moving freely on the streets, not all veiled. I saw what was happening there, and then I went back to the West and saw the media coverage. I was appalled at how biased the coverage was.

So that was one critical moment. The other moment was when I went to the Caribbean in my twenties. I had a Caribbean friend, Marla Bishop, who grew up with us in Kaduna, and we went together to Grenada during the halcyon days of the Grenadian revolution. That was probably the most inspiring moment in the eighties, meeting Maurice Bishop. I was completely captivated by what Bishop and Jacqueline Creft were doing,[4] and the prominence of women in that revolution: the Ministry for Women, the fact that the minister of education was a woman, and all over the island there were colorful political murals—women for freedom, women in defense, women in production—so it was very much a socialist revolution that placed women as very much involved as equal partners. But then the conscientization in terms of global politics was what happened to that revolution. I can remember driving down the Kensington High Street and hearing that Maurice Bishop had been killed. The shattering of that dream was at the time very distressing, devastating.

Now I look back and think those two moments were signs of what was to come in terms of what was happening to left politics and to radical women's organizing in both of those contexts.

Linda E. Carty: Yeah. And it is interesting that at the same time this is when Thatcher and Reagan and neoliberalism took off! They had a vision of what kind of states they wanted.

AM: Absolutely. Thatcherism happened when the violence was breaking out in London—at the same time I was visiting Nigeria, and we had a series of military coups over structural adjustment. Each "corrective regime" was promising not to do SAPs because of the devastating effects it was having on the public sector,[5] which the vast majority of people in Africa depend on for health, education, and water. The economic divide was sharpening. People in Nigeria have always been very conscious. They resisted and fought back against SAPs. The students were out; there was a lot of popular resistance. The military, of course, dealt with that in their own particular way. Each regime—and two in particular[6]—claimed they were *not* going to not impose SAPs, but then they came back with even more draconian measures in the early eighties—the advance of what we now call neoliberalism. The gendered impacts of the constriction of the state were very clear. It was largely through the post-independence public sector that women moved from farming, street-hawking, and trading into professional employments. For example, free public education was critical, and, after all, women were the pioneers of education in Africa as well as its most eager beneficiaries. As the public sector diminished, women were funded to do micro-enterprises and so displaced back into the informal economy.

The second thing, of course, is when all those services got undermined, the burden of all that care work—what we now call the "care economy"—fell on women; women were disposable in the economy, what we used to think of as the "reserve army of labor." We were experiencing the neoliberal economic reforms that were actually piloted in Africa first, during the seventies. Now we can see that it started with the imposition of structural adjustment policies in the seventies. Nowadays African feminists point to the Association of African Women for Research and Development (AAWORD) as our early response to the ways in which modernization and industrialization compounded women's marginalization. There was anti-neoliberal activism beginning on the continent. So there was that link and the global nature of these developments demanded that feminism be more than local. The primary manifestation was around local issues, but the international linkages were easy to pick up on, so Black and Third World feminists continued the conversations about anti-imperialist strategies in the women's movement. It is only later that I can look back and [see] what led me to what is now called a transnational understanding of the forces against women. Challenges to racism informed Black community politics in the diaspora, but what worked for me across my Western and non-Western locations was what we used to call anti-imperialism, and in African circles, pan-Africanism.

CTM: Amina, how would you say that your work has contributed to sustained change in women's lives?

AM: I cannot think about it in terms of "my" work, because all the things that have been of value that I can look back on, or indeed think forward on, have been about developing communities of shared ideas and politics. As an individual, maybe you can write something, but I do not think that does enough that is transformative. Change has really been about working in groups and organizations and creating structures here and there. Why do we make organizations? We make them to do more than what we ourselves can do as individuals. It is only collective action that can make real change.

Speaking as a feminist, in terms of what we've been able to do, I think we have always confronted one particular major challenge that comes from living in an unjust and unequal system, and that is class. Our movements have inequalities within them, because we are formed in conventional, classed societies. Within movements we have to change ourselves as well as achieve things for women. Call me old-fashioned, but the injustice that carries through across all others, and among women, is a radical understanding of *class*, and the perpetual production of systemic, social divisions. Some women (and I have to include myself here) have obviously benefited from what women's movements have done.

In African countries the focus has been on getting women into power, into government. In a few countries we have got large numbers of women in the government. The ensuing debate is about, one, that these women got into power on the back of women's movements, and, two, they are not accountable to us. Even those we might call feminist sympathizers are somehow not effective enough in terms of women's interests, and that has to do with the systems they are trying to work through. Women politicians soon learn that a political career requires alliances and dalliances with the patriarchs—the few Big Men. There is also the fact that when women move into a power structure, they also move up class-wise and tend to disengage with those who protocol now positions "below" them. Of course, we women *should* want power, but I think feminists who become politicians are still working out how to use it for women's interests. But, then, very few feminists can survive as such in the political arenas. One of the most effective feminist politicians I have had the privilege of knowing is Pregs Govender, the South African MP,[7] who carried a feminist agenda into the Parliament, and mobilized people far beyond the Parliament, in order to bring change in the Parliament.

Some of these examples show us what needs to be done. If only all of us paid more attention to them. Yes, you need to get women in power, but also keep alive that continuing connection to collective mobilization *outside* structures that are toxic, quite often inimical to women, and certainly inimical to women who are feminists. By definition, feminists are those women who actually do want to change the world, and who think beyond their own career, family, and personal interests. We have made huge gains, but they have not been enough;

they have not transformed ordinary women's lives. Yet that is what movements inspired by feminism stand for.

The world has been changed by the processes of globalization and neoliberalization; with each advance the fragmentations and divisions have become much sharper. Achievements—like getting women into politics—are undermined when politics loses power. Getting women into the state may not be the most effective strategy when the state no longer has sovereignty. So we have to change that strategy if we want to make a difference. Women without economic means cannot use the new laws against domestic violence, so the burden of care and support services overwhelming many women's organizations does not wither away with legal reform.

The reinstantiation of divisions between women has sabotaged the visionary agendas of feminism, which are about transforming ordinary women's lives. The system has proved a lot tougher and more resilient than any of us could have imagined twenty or even ten years ago. I don't think we ever foresaw the subordination of independent African states to multinational corporate interests or global dominance of US national security doctrine. Yet the radical awareness of the military industrial complex is not new. The military and corporate elite are heavily centered in the West, while the majority of people suffering abjection and despair are still concentrated in the former colonies. We really need to escalate political mobilization to a new level and find new modes of resistance at this time.

CTM: Do you think it has something to do with the kind of feminist ideas that we in the Global South have been able to popularize or not? In other words, one of the things that always strikes me is that in many places we have managed to get certain kinds of powers, certain organizations, and certain institutions in place, but the experience of walking down the street has not changed in many places.

LEC: What have we done with feminism as ideas and theorization in the academy that has not translated to those women? When I go to the Caribbean, and I talk to those women for whatever kind of research I am doing in the region, I hear them say, "Feminism? I don't know what that is, because those women up there"—and they are referring to women in the academy—"they have nothing to do with us. They don't know what I do."

AM: That is true. It is a similar kind of disconnect, whether you are talking about women getting into the parliaments, the obvious site of power, or the academy in which knowledge and truth purportedly reside. Many of us chose the academy because of its potential as a site for conscientizing the next generation. I think we all understand the value of education, particularly in the South. So there is that, but then I also think we need to talk about the role of feminist intellectuals here and look critically (in my case self-critically) at what happens to feminists in the academy. We are very quick to judge and distance ourselves from one another, but we need to reanalyze the structures of power inside the universities as much as any other institution that we inhabit. It is a serious job to try and create a radical intellectual space in the education system, and I've spent many years of my life doing that. I am well aware that for as long as I work in the public university, part of my work is to keep questioning the institution, and repurposing it daily towards serving and validating those not born into power and privilege yet paying the highest taxes.

Why do I work in the university? Today's university is fraught terrain. I moved into the US academy late in my career. It is the furthest I have been from any revolutionary idea of what a university could contribute. Nowadays, African campuses are struggling, but US campuses rely on military and corporate investment. They are still rich to the extent that they are tightly bound into the neoliberal system, and radical thinkers are facing harassment and intimidation. Surveillance is taken for granted, minorities still minorized, while the rhetoric on "embracing difference" and "diversity" gets louder. More than ever we need structures as well as networks that span civil society, feminist and other progressive movements, and which take radical theory and analysis seriously. This is in fact the work we were able to do at the African Gender Institute for about a decade[8]—working to put the politics back into gender studies and women's movements, into both research and into activism, and to bring those together, so they can inform each other. We need to work across institutional and movement sites. There are now women in every sphere who we can say are feminists. Linking up across disciplines, across institutional spaces, and indeed across all kinds of borders, continues to be very challenging.[9] Those with resources may be liberal but unable to comprehend the value of this kind of cross-border work, because it does not echo the institutional or intellectual conventions with which they are familiar. Or they just may be viscerally hostile, disparaging and resenting its authors.

LEC: It speaks to how some of us have kept one foot in the academy and one in the community. You do not want that split, because you understand you want one to impact the other.

AM: That is why we call ourselves "feminist scholars" or "feminist intellectuals," because you are combining the political with the analytical.

LEC: What do you see as one of the best ways across race, ethnicity, class divides as well as within and across national borders to build solidarity in the current climate of neoliberalism and its impact on the Global South?

AM: Building solidarities is primarily a task of conscientization. We have to be constantly in a process of becoming alert to the things that divide and oppress us in historically specific ways, if we are to strengthen an alternative political culture, one that is premised on different kinds of relationships. It is about how we connect. The eighties was a period where identity politics surfaced, necessarily, because of the legacies of racism and classism. Within the women's movement, women from the South added traction by challenging the liberal hegemonies of Western feminism, because the "add women" approach can never work in societies that are intrinsically undemocratic, and divided. Liberal approaches, including conventional approaches to 'women's rights,' can never be adequate to the tasks of decolonization, deracialization, or socialism (the pursuit of social justice) in places that have a history of gross injustice. Women's liberation cannot be attained in isolation, and the myth that it can is divisive.

One of the key challenges we face in African countries is that the feminism has emerged out of different historical conditions, even if we are part of a global order. Nationalism and nationhood were central in the context of twentieth-century imperialism. However, with our imperfect nation-states now severely weakened, we need to really reassess that focus. We used to see the state as the vehicle for getting out from under colonial domination, and then as a bulwark that was supposed to protect us against Western corporate interests. The twenty-first-century questions now are different. We need to ask, Who is benefitting from the demise of the state, not just in Africa, where "corrupt natives" have been blamed, but globally? Who benefits from our eternal indebtedness, from loss of basic social security, or from conflicts that appear to be local? Who benefits from the displacement of sociality by individualism, consumerism, or from the privatization of public assets, and the seizures of public land by private interests? What are the differentiated effects of the militarized extractive industries governing large swaths of the continent?

CTM: Can you think about examples of projects that you are familiar with that you would call radical and that are doing urgent, necessary feminist work in the world?

AM: That is a very important question. It is a tall order too. It is easy to see that the histories, the experiences, and the strategies that have been used so far need to change, are no longer sufficient, as we move forward. The definition of a radical perspective changes with each decade and possibly even faster nowadays. One of the key things that I am currently working on is documenting women's movements through time.

What I see today in women's movements, particularly in Africa, is an awareness of the importance of connecting across age groups.

The need for temporal bridging is not just a matter of there being older and younger people, or older and younger feminists. The thing is that the pace of things has been escalated by neoliberal capitalism. Change does not just happen across generations—from parent to child, mother to daughter, mother to son—but between sisters just a few years apart. One of the exciting things I see in Africa's feminist movements is that a lot of the more established organizations are putting energy into movement building. This means sharing the experience, the consciousness, and the meaning of organizing for change. The limitations of are easy for all to see; indeed we hear these exaggerated all the time in the mainstream social discourse othering "feminists" as elite, out-of-date, and internally there are objections to the misuses of power of older women. When older feminists exercise power in counterproductive ways, call them out! If the modest little organizations that have struggled into existence over the last three decades don't seem "radical" enough to deserve the labor and support of younger women, join the struggle to change them from within, or organize new ones. If the limitations of NGOs as conduits for activism create a sense of frustration, then don't waste energy tearing them down or condemning them for "merely" providing care and services to women, or for struggling to work with allies in government. Devise new strategies and invent other vehicles for protest and activism.

Moving to the US has brought into focus the importance of historical and materialist analysis, because there is such all-consuming preoccupation with issues around identity, and it is the proliferating sexual identities that are dominating the discourse. We need to keep asking, What are the conditions that bring this about?

CTM: And historical amnesia.

AM: Yes, certainly within the Western academy, which is where I am located. It is that concept that you borrowed from Foucault, "the threshold of disappearance." All the talk among students here is *not* about the next stage of radical feminism; it is about the changing LGBT/queer/trans vocabulary. Students are challenging us for even teaching "gender" or "women's" studies, because they are positioning themselves "outside" the heteronormativity, apparently unaware that challenges to heteronormativity are basic to feminist thinking. Politically correct pronouns seem to be more important than correct politics! LGBTQI and A; there is unanimity about what it is to be any of those, because identities are forever in progress. The question is whether we are interested in getting beyond the personal or content to just reducing everything to the personal and personal choices. Self-discovery should really be the first step away from egocentrism and selfishness, not the endpoint! At some point we have to become political in the larger sense.

One thing I would like to do more of is pooling feminist knowledge and insight and sharing these more effectively. That is what I understand the Feminist Freedom Warriors project is about. The journal *Feminist Africa* is about trying to cultivate feminist knowledge in and about African gender politics, and putting it on record so people across decades and generations can see the historicity and power that feminism has in African contests. Creating such spaces is far from easy. One of the things I've had to live with is the realization that some of our best ideas and projects may never happen. It remains hard to mobilize resources to pursue independent feminist projects. This is very tricky terrain in postcolonial contexts that bear perverse legacies of violent, misogynistic, and colonial sexual politics. There are no acronyms or pronouns that can adequately convey the intensely political nature of the struggles feminists wage.

When I think about alternatives, there are many areas where we have not done nearly enough. For example, we have been uncreative with regard to familial structures. Many feminists inhabit patriarchal families. Others adopt the heteronormative nuclear structure while trying to live it in a more just, less exploitative manner. We have not been creative in thinking about socializing child care. As we find ourselves with less time, we need to revisit the questions of domesticity and the care economy. How we can free up time for political work, for relationships, imagination, and activism, without standing on the exploitation of poorer and migrant women and girls?

CTM: Perhaps some of what you are saying is to envision collective structures that push back against the individualist, competitive, and carnivorous values that are very much a part of the time we live in.

LEC: Imagining that another world is out there without just looking to what is right there. For example, challenging the hegemonic paradigm of family that gay and lesbian people are trying to adopt.

AM: We seem to be reenacting the patriarchal family structure, as if no one ever read Engels's *The Origins of the Family.*

LEC: It is really problematic. When you look at the United States' structure, we can understand why that is the case. Without it, LGBT communities will have absolutely no rights, and no access legally, which is not the case in so many other countries, where you do not see people rushing to marry, because they have alternatives and they are acknowledged and recognized by the system. They do not have that here, so there is no other way.

AM: Yes, and some gay couples are transnational couples, where marriage is also about committing to migration. Capital can migrate, but woe betides if you want to bring a partner home. So people marry for that. I ask friends, "Why are you conforming to the patriarchal paradigm of marriage?" and if they were radical feminists, they say, "Well, it's not that we believe in the nuclear family. It's because we want to retire. We want our partner to be able to live with us and share health policy, health insurance." It is very practical, but that is exactly how we are reinserted in the patriarchal order. It is not so easy to adopt a patriarchal family structure and live it differently, because the institution has its own momentum.

We need to transform institutions, from families through community and government structures, all the way up to global governance structures, so that no terrain is neglected. The plus side of that is that you can be an activist wherever you are. This institutional approach is a different idea of activism, very different from social movement approaches, or revolutionary struggles for state power. In a way, maybe this is something that feminism has contributed to the meaning of politics: a deep understanding of the pervasiveness of power and its productivity. Resistance to oppression can and does take root in almost any institution, any oppressive situation. It is down to movements to bring things together, so the will to strengthen movements comes from an optimistic viewpoint.

CTM: That is what keeps many of us going, no?

AM: Well, just think about relationships. We know each other; we can see when we go into any of those movement spaces the energy, the vision, and the creative thought. Things you might expect in the university. Students nowadays are all so stressed over their loans and finances. One of the hardest things to do is to think freely in research universities. What irony!

LEC: Some of our graduate students are facing the dilemma right now of what the institutional agendas are and what to do with your own agenda when the two do not line up.

AM: That is why they need us in there. We are few, but for the students we do take on and work with, we are in a sense their only option, because we are spread way too thin.

LEC: So much in this academy is determined by resources. Funding that they can and cannot get.

CTM: There is a whole history of autonomous universities in various parts of Latin America, coming out of a Freirean model of community education, which is about decolonizing knowledge. We in the academy could really learn from it, but the conditions in the academy are so different that to really learn from it, you have to do a thorough critique of the institution we happen to be in.

LEC: In Latin America they have had some serious struggles, which they have managed to work against. They have kept the state out successfully, and in cases where they seem about to fall apart, they had offers of state funding and they refused so that that work can continue. That is what it will take. The kinds of comforts and resources that we have gotten used to is a real challenge.

AM: At the African Gender Institute, we started with working on the curriculum in the University of Cape Town too soon after the formal end of apartheid. Being a historically white institution, it was also difficult territory. With hindsight, I think that the colleagues there were suffering from trauma. The loss of apartheid, effectively the world's biggest and most extreme affirmative action system ever, left them anxious that they were going to be pushed aside by Black South Africans. Interestingly, we developed a strategy rather like what you and Linda are doing with the Democratizing Knowledge Project,[10] which is to raise money from elsewhere to do the radical intellectual work that we think the university should be doing! To do this requires a community of likeminded people across campuses, outside any specific institution. We set about creating those intellectual spaces in which to develop curriculum, co-teach, and then try to institutionalize the radical teaching ideas in the multiple institutions across which we are scattered. The funding climate has made radical knowledge work, including feminist knowledge work, harder and harder, so we are challenged to find ways of doing it, ways that are not as easily deradicalized as the departmental and disciplinary structures have turned out to be.

One of the pains of the movement is the way in which people would spend twenty or thirty years building an organization and then one bad circumstance can take it down within a matter of days. Witnessing the fragility of structures, and the ease with which they can be crushed or appropriated, has led me away from trying to build within my workplace. Instead, after a number of attempts at radical innovations in educational structures, I have reverted to working with feminist networks, most of which are outside universities, although I am fully employed by a university and maintain a family. The NGO experience has been very productive for women's movements, but still limited. We've learnt that when collectives start NGOs, they are forced to adopt a particular hierarchical structure, either because donors want an individual, not a committee, or because governments require registration on the same terms. It is hard to create institutions of our own design and intent. Networks also have limitations when it comes to engaging with power structures. Yet it is not easy to organize and pursue radical projects within market-driven institutions.

What are other ways in which we can work collectively? Individuals cannot bring about change on their own, so we need to appreciate the importance of having organizations and resources that can *support* organizing, even if their formal existence is about service provision. I think feminist NGOs have been onto this for a long time. The real objective is to change people, and my hope is that we are doing this more effectively that we realize.

Further Reflections:
Imagining a Revolutionary Feminist Politics

AM: Reflecting on the current global scenario, it strikes me that the commonalities between developed and underdeveloped nations are becoming clearer than they have been for a while. Africans mostly pursued political independence and ended colonial occupation in order to become nations like other nations. The first decade of political independence energetically pursued modernization programs to this end, only to find themselves mired in deepening dependency and indebtedness, accompanied by authoritarian regimes that see-sawed between grace and disparagement among their powerful international benefactors and detractors. Post the Cold War, decades of economic reform have also not led to the envisaged fraternity of nations. Instead we have a global web of corporate interests backed up by a global security system, both working to transform life and the planet in ways hitherto seen on the sets of dystopic sci-fi films.

In the African Union, as in the USA, the beneficiaries of the residualized state are the rich, and their lives are organized around private schools, private health care, and air-conditioned SUVs with darkened windows. In Lagos, as in Kingston, the inconveniences of infrastructural decline are now so advanced that even the poorly paid professional class have to invest in backyard boreholes, and internet access requires a generator. Like US citizens, many citizens of African nations are born into indebted nations, where poor people are taxed disproportionally higher than the super-rich.

However, there is no doubt that the enforcement of free market economics has had its most negative effects in already weak markets. Millions of Africa's people are enmeshed in poverty, without health insurance or any other safety net. What desperation drives people to clamber onto dinghies and take their chances crossing the Mediterranean, knowing that thousands before them have drowned? How have decades of poverty alleviation and sustainable development sustained so much poverty? Why are growing security budgets not improving security? What is peace where peacekeepers buy a child's body for a piece of bread? In any case, what does "security" mean for women farmers scratching at increasingly desiccated land? Livelihoods are precarious, quality of life indexed by peacetime life expectancies in the forties and fifties, and survival is not guaranteed at any age. There are no indicators that can convey what life is like in such places. But nor do indicators tell us the flavors of the food, the love people have for one another, or the vivid beauty of landscapes that extend to thousands of miles as yet ungrabbed. These are lands where, despite such extreme contradictions, women walk with straight backs, and children invent toys with old tires and metal wires. These are the fringes of neoliberal empire.

The contrast between the mass movements of the past and the civil society of today has deep implications for the politics of what is possible with regard to democratization in general and feminist agendas in particular. In practical terms, the liberal interest in building civil society in Africa has translated into funding for NGOs. Women's NGOs—most of them small-scale—proliferated across the continent from the 1980s onwards, in a climate further sweetened by the UN Decade for Women. (This does not mean that women are fairly represented in the NGO sector. On the contrary, there is evidence that the NGO community as a whole exhibits the same gross underrepresentation of women in leadership positions as state and corporate sector organizations.)[11]

Pan-African feminist networks were formed during the same period to address issues on a continental scale. Among the best known is FEMNET, the pan-African, feminist Women's Communication and Development Network, established in 1988. FEMNET records over five hundred organizational and individual members across forty-three countries and has become a highly effective advocate in international forums, particularly the African Union. During the same era a series of women's legal rights networks—among them the African Women in Law and Development (WILDAF) network, extending to twenty-six focal offices across the continent, and Women and Law in Southern Africa—made major contributions to legal research that informed struggles for more just inheritance and maintenance laws. Others took on the challenges surrounding women's sexual and reproductive rights.

The value of the significant work carried out by women's movements through their organizations needs to be appreciated in the face of the sustained barrage of criticism levied at women suspected of feminism. The leadership and staff—most of them women—are routinely disparaged for having well-educated professional profiles that would be highly valued in almost any other context. Women's NGOs are also dismissed as "donor-driven," a charge that grossly underestimates the agency and strategic acumen of those who carry out women's movement work through NGOs. The truth is that through NGOs, women's movements have been able to pursue certain kinds of work over the last three decades: education, training and outreach projects, antiviolence work, legal advice, counseling, and support services. In many countries they carry out the extensive lobbying and advocacy work through which women have engaged the state and, often successfully, pushed for legal and policy changes.

Women have established hundreds of NGOs to respond to the harsh realities of women's lives in the region.[12] Women's NGOs have

provided decent work and career development for the rapidly growing pool of educated women at a time when the public-sector education, training, and welfare provisions were being retracted, limiting
the already limited space for the employment of women. The majority
of NGOs have remained small and under-resourced, able to employ
only small numbers of staff to work extremely hard on salaries below
market rate, and with very limited budgets. Others may employ a
dozen or more staff, and most run sophisticated operations. Women
working in African women's NGOs contribute countless hours of
unpaid voluntary labor, actually *subsidizing* donor funds. But, then,
most of them are women, working with and for women, so contrary
to allegations, this is seldom just about salaries. It's also about relationships, about sisterhood.[13] At the same time, the struggle to secure
and maintain even the most modest offices has been arduous enough
to have taken a toll on a generation of dedicated activists.

In recent years, feminists in many African countries are leading
the way with regard to building coalitions across civil society, with
communities, traditional institutions, and local political structures, in
order to mount effective campaigns. One example is that of the Domestic Violence Coalition in Ghana, which from 2001 on mounted
a highly effective national campaign and engaged the government for
several years to push for a Domestic Violence Act, eventually passed
in 2007. Another is the Nigeria women's movement's success at stav-
ing off the attempt to introduce an Indecent Dressing Bill in 2008.
Feminists on a list that includes Botswana, Tanzania, and Ghana have
led Women's Manifesto processes, using coalition building to carry
out nationwide consultations and generate national policy platforms,
aiming these at governments and political parties taking gender politics beyond the ranks of the women's movements.

Building broader constituencies for change is hard work, and the
work of NGOs can never approach the scale that would typify a basic
government program. However, over the last three decades, the wom-
en's movements on the continent have continued to grow, and countless
thousands, possibly millions, of women have benefited from the work
of women's NGOs. When major campaigns succeed, and thousands

turn out to join national actions, it indicates that the work of women's NGOs, while it is not easily quantified, has been bringing about quiet, long-term changes in popular consciousness, but this broader societal change becomes apparent only during moments of mobilization.

The global landscape affords African governments very little credibility, yet they are still the primary funders of development in most nations. However, working with government requires particular networks and a skill set that is different from that required to run organizations, work with women, or engage with donors. Despite the manifest resistance of government functionaries to treat women's movements as partners, disengaging has never been a realistic option. Indeed, with all the limitations of our governments, it is in relation to the state that feminist activism in Africa has seen the most significant results. With democratization, things do change. We have seen how modest, well-organized demonstrations of a thousand women can create public debate and shift consciousness, as well as pressure government, by combining protests with media strategies and advocacy.[14] Feminist activists surviving neoliberalism in Africa have developed a remarkable level of strategic sophistication and skill, both on the ground in local contexts and on the international landscapes.

The installation of Donald Trump as president of the USA adds a new level of precariousness to the global landscape. Feminism itself emerged out of precariousness—the systemic precariousness imposed by patriarchy that forever defines women in terms of their gender and their sexuality, and subjects us to the dictates of others, and the precariousness of the global market for the 99 percent. Feminists will meet the challenges of today's unreasonable men with the same stoicism and defiance as that during colonial rule, national liberation wars, dictatorships, and multiparty electoral games. We always find new ways to think and learn, to gather ourselves and unlock our visions, and to find the material resources to continue the struggle for freedom of women, for African women, for Africans, and for Africa.

Photo by Richard Cisneros

Searching for Truth in Community

Aída Hernández-Castillo

Coming of Age: Aída's Story

Aída Hernández-Castillo: I am part of a generation of Mexican feminists like many of my friends that arrived at feminism through the left. We started to be activists mainly in the anti-systemic struggle of the eighties, when Central America was very important in our struggle. When I was seventeen years old I arrived in Mexico City to study social anthropology, and I became involved in the movement of solidarity with Guatemala. I was working for the Guatemalan press agency that was called Enforensa at the time. My first years of political activism were very linked to the struggle in Central America, more specifically in Guatemala. I started to get involved politically but very close to a sector of the left that was very critical of institutional politics. I was only seventeen; I was very young.

Each of us had a political adviser (*responsable politico* was the term we used in Spanish) who were our political teachers within the political organization, and they were very concerned with feminism being an ideology that divides people. It was a very masculine Che Guevara kind of ethics. In those times the women in academia that declared themselves feminist were upper-middle-class women who were very centered on their struggle in the pro-choice agenda. I did not identify myself with these kinds of women. At the same time the struggle that was a priority for us was the genocide of indigenous people in Guatemala. So the pro-choice agenda was the last of my concerns. For many years I was not a feminist. I could even say that I was anti-feminist, because I was against that limited feminist agenda.

When I finished my undergraduate studies, I moved to Chiapas. I started to work in the refugee camps there, and I got very involved with the Maya indigenous women that were Guatemalan refugees. We were working with popular education methodology, trying to figure out how to create a critical consciousness, but also how to build a community in exile. I became a very good friend with another woman who studied education at Universidad Nacional Autónoma de México [National Autonomous University of Mexico]. She was my roommate. In 1988 she was kidnapped by federal police and gang-raped. This experience marked my life. When she came back home, we went to the legal authorities, the Ministerio Público—the public attorney—and the way she was treated by the justice bureaucrats was awful. Somebody told us that she was not the only case of sexual violence by security forces that had occurred in those days, so we put an advertisement on the local radio inviting women that had had any problems with sexual violence and did not find justice in the state legal system to get together in a coffeehouse in San Cristóbal de Las Casas. Around seventy women arrived. Some of them had been raped by police forces, others by their own relatives; some were indigenous women that had been expelled by the political bosses (*caciques*) of their communities after being raped. We had to move to a house because there was not enough space in the coffeehouse. This was the beginning of the first feminist organization in which I participated. I realized that it was very difficult to continue working for social justice without considering what we now call "intersections"—the effects of different systems of violence that we were experiencing. But it took a long time for me to declare myself a feminist.

We created an organization that was called Grupo de Mujeres de San Cristóbal de Las Casas, and we had a women's shelter that was self-sustained with our own personal funding. Indigenous and non-indigenous women worked together, some of them from Mexico City, some from Chiapas. Many of the feminist decolonial theories that we are now discussing came to my heart and mind through my practice in those years, because I saw that political activism centered on class, and antistate struggle was not considering race and gender; it was leaving something out. A lot of methodologies that we were using against violence were methodologies that we took from the experiences of feminist organizations in Mexico City. For example, our main strategy was a legal strategy using the state justice institutions, and many of the women that came to our shelter were indigenous women that were dealing with customary law in their communities. And we had a team of feminist lawyers that knew nothing about customary law. I started to challenge the ways in which the feminist strategies we were using were not responding to the specific needs of a very diverse cultural area in which we lived. In that search I found Chandra's work, among other feminist readings by women of color, and thought about how it was another form of colonialism to go to a place and say that "we all have to do this or that." We were all volunteers at that time. For example, the lawyer was a very ethnocentric lawyer, and she probably had a racist attitude towards many of the women that came to the shelter; she considered the cultures they were from as backward cultures. But at the same time, she had been working for free for them for fifteen years. It is not that easy just to dismiss her work.

Chandra Talpade Mohanty: Because these are also people who are working and have given labor without recognition for a long time. But what you are talking about, Aída, is more so. While we want to acknowledge the integrity of individuals who are doing this work with the best of intentions, there is a disconnect between what they are doing and what they see as good work, and what the larger collective or community actually needs the work to be like, especially if you reproduce colonial paradigms. This is why knowledge is so dangerous sometimes.

AHC: So how can we build bridges? I always say to my friends that good theory helps good practice, and that having a more complex perspective of how those intersections work helps us to look for various strategies. Because if what we want is a better life for the women with whom we work, we do not want to gain legal cases. That should not be the main objective but the well-being of the women. You can gain a case, and when the woman goes back to her community, she is isolated or stigmatized because she did not consider the elders or the communitarian justice system; she just went to the state law. So we have to see what kind of strategies we can build.

We have something to offer from academia to these kinds of projects. I proposed to them a workshop in which indigenous women who worked in accompanying cases of domestic violence and who were, for example, rural teachers, nurses, or midwives (because women that are victims of domestic violence usually go to those women that have some kind of power in the community) could teach our legal team how customary law was treating those cases. The legal team would then teach this group of women how to make a legal case if they wanted to go to the state law. The proposal was to have a dialogue of knowledge about different legal systems to search for intercultural strategies towards justice for women. I did not know anything about the state law or customary law, so for me it was a learning experience on both sides.[1]

CTM: Was this still in Chiapas?

AHC: Yes. In the end they decided to create a network of antiviolence women´s rights promoters among women of different communities. Many of them were from different indigenous groups and regions, so they worked in isolation, a context that makes them very vulnerable. Because in many cases, getting involved in a case of domestic violence of somebody else is considered in their communities as just being gossipy. So the network gave them some protection; they were less isolated in their defense of women's rights.

With the lawyers it was more difficult, because the lawyers' community is very close-minded; I always say they are like a closed ethnic group. They have their language, and it is very difficult for them to decenter the rule of law as the center of their strategy. I am still working with lawyers a lot, and I have another goal now to try to bring the discussion on legal pluralism and decolonial feminist thinking to the law schools.

More recently, many feminists in Latin America, and in Mexico specifically, have been arguing about how customary law can be against women's rights. They have spent a lot of time struggling against customary law, while at the same time state law, the penal law, is putting a lot of women in prison. There is very little energy left to deal with the problem of imprisonment.

After many years of working with issues that were related to customary law, eight years ago I began to work with the issue of penal law and what I call *racismo judicial*—judicial racism—that is, how racism has marked the access to justice for a racialized woman in Mexico. It is a collective project. What happened is that we were struggling with the issue of customary law because in 2001 there was a law reform in Mexico that recognized the rights of indigenous people to their own justice system. Many feminists started to scream publicly that such a recognition meant going backwards in women's rights, that it would open the possibility for women's rights to be violated by indigenous justice systems. In this debate they barely included the voices of indigenous women. They rarely included the multiple experiences of indigenous women that are participating in the transformation of their justice system. It became like the Muslim and the veil. They do not call it the "indigenous justice system," but "uses and customs."

We started this project to try to see what women were doing with their own justice system. I worked with a beautiful team of female legal anthropologists from CIESAS [Center for Research and Advanced Studies in Social Anthropology] that had been working together for a long time (María Teresa Sierra, Mariana Mora, and Rachel Sieder). But when we were working on this project, there was a huge issue with the repression of a peasants' movement that wanted to stop the construction of an airport in communal lands—the Atenco movement.[2] The police repressed the movement, and seventeen women were raped and put into jail. This event became a scandal because two of the women were foreigners and they gave their testimony of the rapes. It took me to jail for the first time. I went to visit them in jail. One of them was an indigenous woman who was a street vendors' organizer who was at this meeting, supporting the demands of the people of Atenco; her name was Magdalena Garcia Duran. Amnesty International termed her a political prisoner. When I was there I realized there were many indigenous women that were not political prisoners in the strictest sense but that were prisoners of a state policy against drugs that is criminalizing small vendors (*narco menudeo*), people that sell small quantities of drugs and get very high penalties, ten to fifteen years. I started this new stage of my activism and my scholarly work, because I wanted to see who those women were and to document the structural racism of the penal system.

To get entry into the jail was very difficult. I found a feminist poet, Elena de Hoyos, who was teaching creative writing in one of the jails in the Mexican state of Morelos, so I entered through her. I wanted to write the life stories of those women in prison, and one of the writers, an inmate with a Korean background, Suzuki Lee Camacho, told me, "They don't allow you to enter and they don't allow us to go out. We are writers. Why don't you teach us how to write life stories? And we can interview the other inmates and write their stories." This was the beginning of a project that really had a great impact on my life. For eight years I have been working with them. From the first book given to me that was written by hand, we have come a long way; they have written and published twelve books. I helped to correct that first book; that was the result of a dialogue between indigenous and mestizo inmates. I got funding for a publication called *Under the Shadow of the Guamúchil.*[3]

They decided that they wanted to learn to make books and not just to write them. Marina Ruiz, a feminist editor, started to work with us. She is part of a movement that does art-craft books with recycling materials. She taught a workshop on that. A group was formed from that workshop, the Colectiva Editorial de Mujeres en Prisión Hermanas en la Sombra (Editorial Collective of Women in Prisons, Women in the Shadows).[4] They write the books, they capture the texts; the entire editorial process is now under their control. We bought two computers. We have a radio program. Inmates that are out continue to be part of the collective. Now part of the struggle is how to impact public policy towards prisons. They are working on that. I have many doubts, because the state is so corrupt. I find it very difficult to imagine that part of my struggle will be for public policy. I prefer more grassroots movements, but there is a sector of the collective that wants to do that.

Linda E. Carty: Because they probably recognize if you can make some kind of positive, progressive change at the level of policy, you can impact so much more. Sometimes we tend to think at the level of grass roots more. We understand how intense that is and how impactful it can be in small time. Working with the state, that is such an organized, intransigent bureaucracy, it is easy to become hopeless because they will not change very easily.

AHC: In Mexico the state is so linked to organized crime. The people that you deal with as bureaucrats can also be part of a cartel, so it is very difficult. Something else that happens very easily is that they pass repressive laws and then use progressive laws that have to do more with cultural politics to distract public opinion from the repressive legislation. They even pass the two kinds of laws at the same time. This just happened two weeks ago. On the Day Against Homophobia, the president of Mexico promoted a law advancing LGBT rights and legalizing same-sex marriage. It was a big issue in all the newspapers. The presidential palace was tinted with rainbow colors, and radical activists of the LGBT movement were taking pictures of themselves with the president, Enrique Peña Nieto, with the presidential palace behind them. That same week the president sent a law to Congress in which he gave the military the right to enter into many civilians' issues. It is this game in which you think that you are getting something, but you do not know whether you are really advancing in your struggle for justice or if you are being used.

CTM: The law that was passed was really a law that gives impunity to the state and the military to walk in and criminalize a whole set of actions that may not have been seen as criminal behavior before.

AHC: When the army commits an illegal act or violates human rights with a civilian, they have to be judged by civilian law. With the new legislation, the army members are going back to their military courts. For example, if the army thinks that a civilian is involved in some criminal act that has to do with the army, they can interview the civilian; they can take them to their military camp. So we are losing ground again. That law that made this legal was passed in the same week as all the discourse on sexual diversity—on the seventeenth of May 2016. When I say that sometimes it is very difficult to try to impact state institutions, it is not that I am completely against the idea of working for changes in public policy, because in Latin America as well as the United States, there is a big split between what is called "institutional feminism" and radical feminism, and they have been struggling for a long time. It is not that I have a principle that I would never work with institutions. Rather, the issue is, What kind of institutions do we have when we have a state that works like the Mexican state does in this specific historical moment?

LEC: One of the questions that we have is about what kinds of challenges you have encountered in the work, and you have laid out enormous challenges. What have been some of the strategies you have tried, not just personally but collectively with the groups that you work with, to overcome some of these challenges?

AHC: There are many things. I am part of a network that is called La Red de Feminismos Descoloniales.[5] We are several scholar-activists and we are trying to work more with media. I have a column in a national newspaper called *La Jornada*, in which I write a monthly article on issues related to gender violence and women's struggles for justice.[6] We are trying to use more multimedia. There is a feminist TV channel on the internet. The program is called *Luchadoras* (Fighters)[7], which has opened its space to our network. We are trying to diversify the textual strategies that we use to go beyond the book. That is one area in which we are working.

The other area is political alliances, which is a big challenge all over. There is a lot of tension in Mexico over political alliances, because recently more people have died in the "war against drugs" in Mexico than in the war in Iraq. Violence and disappearance are the main problems in Mexico. We have to work with the parents of the disappeared, men and women, and many of them are not feminists. For example, the forty-three students from Ayotzinapa that disappeared came from a leftist teacher's culture that has a discourse, practice, and performance that is very "Che Guevara style."[8] Many feminists do not want to work with them. I think there is a moment in which we must articulate our differences, when we have to confront the issue of state violence and the narco state.

As feminists, for example, one issue that we have to deal with is that the people that are linked to drug issues, like many of the inmates, are women who are very vulnerable because nobody wants to defend somebody that can be linked to a cartel. So if you are a feminist, you are not going to use your energy to work with these women. You will prefer to work with political prisoners or with the issue of criminalization of abortion. Nobody wants to get involved with issues of drugs—not the human rights organizations, not the feminist organizations. The majority of women that are being killed or that are in prison are women that did not have choices. The cartels go to communities, kidnap women, and they are forced to go. Many times, when the police capture a criminal group, the group "sacrifices" the women and leaves. Let me explain it: If the police capture a criminal group, which includes, say, three women, the group hands over three women and money to the police, and it leaves. So the men who were responsible for getting the women involved are free, while the women are in prison.

It is very difficult to have sensitivity towards this kind of situation for many reasons. One of them is that the images of what the cartels have done are very bloody, and you do not want to get involved with them at all. If those women were linked in any way to the cartels, you do not want to get close to them. However, now I know them by name. I know their life stories, I know how they were captured and how vulnerable they are, and it is not just those that are in prison. The feminicide rate in Mexico is very high, and many of the women killed were women that were captured, taken away, and then murdered. This is a moment in which human rights organizations and feminist organizations have to build alliances. Right now we are living in a situation of emergency, and we need to build bridges among different social struggles. There are contexts in which you might say, "Ah, no, this Che Guevara–style man, I don't want to work with him. I'm sick of him. I have done it before. I don't want to deal with him." But in a situation of emergency we need to deal with our differences and build something. After the Ayotzinapa case, we have been working a lot trying to get together with different kinds of groups. What are we going to do together? How can we build this? That is my work now.

LEC: What kind of feminist work is being done with the women in prison? For example, the captured group pays for the crime with three women and some money. Something must happen in the minds of those women after they are incarcerated, and they have been there for a long time, and they are thinking about how they were discarded and how they became like objects. On the left we used to say in the old days that when people go to work in the same environment it conscientizes the workers. Some kind of conscientization probably happens to those women. Is there any hope of working with the incarcerated women?

AHC: In the case of the Colectiva Hermanas en la Sombra, that is the work we have been doing for eight years. The writing at the beginning, in the first book they published, was a genealogy of violence. It was about how they suffered; how they were raped as children, then raped as teenagers; how they were abused by their husbands, raped by the police, and tortured in jail. It was just violence, violence, and violence. After they took all the violence out, they started to write about empowerment, building community, and what it means to be together, using poetry but also playing with words in different ways. They have a book of poetry and one of narratives that talks a lot about the experience of building a community and what it means when you discover that you are not alone. They have many books now that are about consciousness raising or consciousness awareness. Conscientization is happening—not everywhere, but many of the incarcerated women are building community. A project that they are working on with a non-inmate member of the *colectiva*, Carolina Corral, a visual anthropologist, is an animated short film about romantic love and the dangers of romantic love. It is entitled *Amor Nuestra Prisión* (Love: Our Prison). It is very funny. They are working on a draft. Some of the members of the *colectiva* that are outside right now are working in other prisons, taking the methodology of building community in prison.

CTM: What is interesting, though, about this project and the early project in Chiapas are some of the threads there are about coming together across various forms of differences—class, ethnicity, dispossession, wealth, professionalization, and other kinds of peasant experiences—and actually finding ways to build community and culture. Part of the critique of why the "Che Guevara–ism" and other forms of left social movements and organizing do not work is because there is not enough attention paid to the kinds of cultures that social movements generate. If those cultures end up being profoundly violent, masculinist cultures, they automatically alienate groups of people. But when you come across differences, sit around a table, and create certain things together—like in this project, when people write poetry and create a video together, or in the earlier project, when people across divides actually teach each other what forms of justice are seen as the right forms of justice—there is a new culture that is created, which is about how you sustain each other. And you do not have to become each other. Audre [Lorde] used to say you do not have to become each other in order to work together, but in order to work together you have to actually do something more than just mobilize against external violence and structural injustice; you have to build something together.[9]

AHC: I have an anecdote from this project that relates to that. The first book they published is called *Under the Shadow of the Guamúchil.* Guamúchil is the only tree in the jail. Everything is cement, and there was one tree. All the rural women and the indigenous women were under the shadow of the Guamúchil doing art-crafts. There is no middle class there. All the urban women with some kind of schooling were taking the courses, seminars, and yoga classes, because there are many things happening in jail. We decided to do the writing workshop under the shadow of the Guamúchil. That is where we got together. Many of them had never been together in the same space in jail, because inside the jail it is very segregated. People that have more schooling would be able to take more courses and would be more interested in those kinds of things. The way we worked is that the women worked with each other during the week, telling the story, and one person was writing it. Once a month we read aloud a story. Reading aloud was a moment of community building. You can tell a story to somebody, but when you listen aloud to your own story being read by this other person, it is a very emotional moment. It was also an opportunity to discuss issues of racism within the jail, because part of the stories were about how a woman felt when she arrived here and she did not speak Spanish and everybody was making fun of her.

In these rituals of community building, two urban women asked the rural women for forgiveness for the way they had treated the rural women before. In Mexico we do not use the word "racism" a lot. They more easily say "discrimination." But the notion that if you are an indigenous rural woman, you have a "backward culture" is a racist issue. The women came to a point where they could finally say, "We can share our differences, but we also see our own violence, the way we have exercised violence against all others that are different than us." In the end some of their books had to do with their life stories but also with their dialogues. What does it mean for me to be able to talk to you? What do I learn from you? They were able to write what they wanted, and in the middle they said, "Well, I always thought that I had suffered a lot, and now I realize how privileged I have been even when I am here," and they started off discussing.

You are right. A very important part for political mobilization is to be able to build community. A community of solidarity is a big challenge, because the foundation of many of these neoliberal states is to individualize, divide, and split. Now there is a huge debate in Latin America (and there was a conference organized by some activists as well) about the commons that goes beyond the indigenous communities,[10] because in Latin America there has always been a link between communality, the common areas and rural areas. There are ongoing efforts in urban areas strategizing how to rebuild these commons. Jail seems like one of the spaces that is totally against solidarity and the commons, but there are things going on in those spaces too.

LEC: The individualism of neoliberalism creates divisions, and we have to figure out how to cross those divisions. We create collectivity, and out of that we get community that creates collective action on some level. The old leftist model of what I will now call Guevara-ism made that really effective. There are all these communities that can come together under a shared knowledge and understanding of who the enemy is, and the enemy is the ruling class. That has been very effective moving across divisions, because there is one central enemy. If we understand that, then we are all working towards something that can benefit everybody. But with individualism there is no possibility of having a collective action. You can have little collectivities here and there, but you cannot have something larger. The work of groups of inmates you described is effective and powerful. It is phenomenal that these women are writing such books in prison.

What is your hope of that becoming something larger? How do we get it beyond where it is now? The question is not for you personally but something larger that I am thinking about, because as an old-guard leftist I see what the positives were, but I completely disagreed with how they worked. I felt disgusted that there was no understanding of the woman question. Even when we tried to engage that, we had to confront many things. I see the failures of feminism in that way.

AHC: Before I answer your question, I want to articulate another challenge. As you said, before, we knew who the enemy was. The intellectual or the activist knew the right message that he or she wanted to bring to the collective space of popular education, and there was a lot of epistemological arrogance in that attitude. It was a truth that he/she had, that he/she would bring to that space to raise the consciousness of those people. It was a great group of very committed people, but there were many things going on in that exchange. With many of these decolonial critiques to ourselves as intellectuals, one issue is that my truth as a feminist of what is emancipation and what is justice is not necessarily what they imagine or what they want. So to arrive to the space of encounter, open to a dialogue in which I am willing to destabilize my certainties, is not as powerful as arriving with "the truth." It is a lot easier to get there with "the truth" than to get there and say, "Well, I just want to see what can we build."

We have been struggling for years to have a better law against domestic violence, and they do not give a damn about that law, because they do not want their husbands to be in jail for fifteen years instead of two. They want them to work in the community, doing something else. It makes us less powerful as activists, because, at least in my case, I feel that I do not want to go there to share "truth." I want to go there to search together. That makes the figure of the activist less appealing than when you go there with something to share.

I always say that the first step will be to be able to destabilize your certainties and be humble enough to say, "Well, I'm searching." And how do we go from the local to the global? I think those are the big challenges. I was invited to Peru by the University of Social Movements,[11] which is being promoted among other people by Boaventura de Sousa Santos.[12] It is linked to the World Forum but is not a university of the World Forum. Their goal is to bring together people from different social movements—graffiti kids, feminists, Afro-American, autonomous Basque people, and anarchists—to share their struggles and strategies for struggle and to discuss with scholars their differences of activist research work within those movements. For the scholar the question is, Can you translate your knowledge to a language in which social movements can feel identified? What can scholars learn from them? It entails challenging their pedagogical training, and it involves getting together and talking to see what can you do.

There is a breadth of people, from people that are religious, to the anarchist Basque that are very secular and antireligion, to young people that feel that the old popular education methodologists are passé and you have to do graffiti or something in-your-face. It is a challenge, but at least these efforts are happening now. It did not happen when we had our leader that hid the "truth." Now at least we can try to listen and learn to recognize. For example, something interesting happened in an encounter there. One of the elders, a Maya man, who was very active in Guatemala, said, "I never imagined that not liking gay people was hate."

CTM: What is important about this is that it sets up encounters that normally do not get set up. Part of the impact of neoliberalism is to tell us that these are all separate struggles, and to not make it possible, in terms of resources and geographies, for people to talk to each other about any of this. We do get together, and we are hoping that people see what it means to talk about the intersectionality of social movements. We have a long way to go, because mostly people are speaking from their spaces. But if everybody is there in good faith to both speak and listen, then you are right—exactly this kind of impact can happen, and it can happen with individuals who have power in their own social spaces and social movements. So there is a potential here for building, if nothing else, a culture of people who are hearing the way people who are very different from them are engaged in fights for freedom and justice. There is potential to actually approach and strategize what it is they need to do, because most of the time those kinds of people don't get together. For example, we have feminist conferences where people who identify as feminist come together, and we have the left forum, where almost no feminists end up. So those things are very separate.

AHC: If we could, as scholars in those spaces, explain that the common enemy—that is, this neoliberal capitalist system—is also built with gender inequalities and colonial legacies, then people might see how my struggle becomes your struggle, because if we do not consider racism, we cannot do anticapitalistic work. The issue in those encounters is not only that I have to have solidarity with your struggle, but to be able to see how our struggles are so embedded, and to show it, besides just saying "intersectionality."

LEC: Show that they're interlinked to the impact on each of us, and all of us, simultaneously.

CTM: Which will then make it a common enemy as well, but a complicated common enemy.

LEC: Because the common enemy then would be within, and not without. It is easier to mark the common enemy without. It is work we would all have to do and *must* do to move to the next step. Aída, looking at what has happened—what you have experienced, the work you have done, what you have lived—and then, looking forward, what kind of society do you envision as tomorrow in Mexico and beyond for women?

AHC: One of the main issues now, besides neoliberalism, is violence. I live in a rural community outside the city of Cuernavaca that has been taken by the cartels. For the last five years, I have been losing people that I care about. A few weeks before I came here my swimming teacher was killed. He was the teacher of my son since a young age, and he was an Olympic swimmer in his youth, and now in his seventies he created a community project to teach local kids to swim.

He was a man that was making a difference in our community, and he was killed resisting a kidnapping.

One of the ideal things that I would like to see is a different kind of society, not just a different kind of state. The sad thing is that this violence has permeated daily life. We have young people killing young people. The community where I live is called Ocotepec. In the late seventies and eighties it was an experiment of the liberation theology to build autonomy, based on ideas of an ecclesiastical community of faith that used the Bible as a tool for social critique. There was a very well known leftist bishop, in the 1970s, Sergio Mendez Arceo, who lived there. He promoted the construction of community, because the best social project of the progressive church is building community, getting people together to read the Bible. You do a critique of the system but also a critique of your life.

One of the reasons I decided to move to this community was because of this history and this genealogy. I bought a house there, and now some of the granddaughters and grandsons of these people are involved with the cartels. Many of them have killed people at fourteen or have been killed. I panic and I ask, How did we lose this collective memory in two generations? What happened? I was interviewing one of the elders one day, and he asked me, "What we did wrong, that we were not able to transmit our values?" Many of those kids, whose parents were poor, are doing those things not out of need or extreme poverty. It is the need for consumption of certain kinds of goods they could not consume. The kind of goods that the media is promoting as "important good to be somebody."

I would like to see a Mexico in which we can recover the values of dignity and respect for life, in which we can build community together in difference, in which towns like Ocotepec can recover its memory and its legacy of community building. Of course the challenge is a lot bigger than changing the men that govern my country. It goes to the daily life of people. What kinds of values are there? What kind of conception of life and death is there? How can we build respect for the difference between urban and rural, between mestizo and indigenous? We cannot go out to a public space after five o'clock. How can we recover this? When I was interviewing this elder, he was almost crying, saying, "How can we put this knowledge of those people that built community in the past as a valuable inheritance for the new generations that are here?"

CTM: It is such a poignant way of talking about building new publics when the physical space itself is unavailable because of the everyday violence. Some of the work we are doing is around creating new publics and communities that believe in different values and in a different conception of what it means to be a human being and treat other people with dignity and compassion.

LEC: It seems like what is missing is having a value for life of your own and others. There is such an intense focus on materiality. It reminds me, there are so many little countries in the Caribbean where people are breaking into people's homes just to get what they have.

AHC: I am very concerned and sad about the lack of respect to life and to your own life. Many of those young men have learned since very young that their life has no value, so they can risk their life for an iPhone. If they lose, they die; if they don't, they have an iPhone. They are willing to take many risks, because the sense of time and the sense of history are missing.

Further Reflections:
Imagining a Revolutionary Feminist Politics

AHC: I want to conclude this dialog with a message of optimism and hope for the new generations of feminists who confront the old and new patriarchal practices as well as a more violent and militaristic world. It becomes difficult to do this when we are before the resurgence of right-wing populist nationalisms, which intend to take us back decades in terms of the recognition of women's rights and politics in favor of social justice. However, it is precisely in such moments as we are experiencing now that it is fundamental to maintain the hope that it is possible to construct other worlds. It is before the imposition of this dystopia that it becomes urgent to build a politics of solidarity among distinct social movements.

Along the breadth and width of the continent, women have mobilized before the right-wing evolution of the nation-states, showing that the feminist movement is a struggle for life and for the survival of the planet. An overview of America—that we have to remember: it is a continent and not a country—we see that the last three years have been marked by the arrival of the right wing into national governments and by women's resistance to these new patriarchal politics. The triumph of Mauricio Macri in Argentina in November of 2015 initiated the cycle of feminist's mobilizations in South America to defend the achievements of the last decades. This right-wing government has initiated the dismantling of social policies in favor of women, thus it disappeared governmental programs and reduced educational and research budgets with respect to gender issues.

Under the slogan #NotOneMore, a wide movement of diverse women has been organized to combat the dismantling of women's health programs, the closing of shelters for victims of gender violence, and the designation of Supreme Court judges who are the enemies of the legalization of abortion, among many other demands. Similar mobilizations took place in Brazil, where the patriarchal coup d'état against President Dilma Rousseff in August 2016 revealed to the public the misogynist and violent nature of the Brazilian right wing. The process of impeachment itself can be considered as sexist and discriminatory, since the representatives who voted against Dilma Rousseff committed irregularities with public funds and are not being investigated for corruption.

One of the most emblematic moments of the impeachment occurred when a right-wing representative dedicated his vote against President Rousseff to Colonel Carlos Alberto Brilhante Ustra, torturer and rapist during the military dictatorship, thus mocking the experiences of torture and sexual violence that the ex-president experienced when she was a political prisoner in the 1970s. Brazilian women are now being governed by a cabinet of white men, headed by the temporary president Michel Temer. This new government has proposed to reverse the political achievements of the feminist movement through projects that define the family as a union of one man, a woman, and their children, prohibiting the discussion of gender in the National Plan of Education and criminalizing abortion for victims of rape and for those who have contracted the Zika virus, as well as eliminating programs of social development and prevention of violence directed toward women.

A similar process was experienced in 2009 in Honduras, when President Manuel Zelaya was demoted during a "soft coup d'état" headed by the National Congress and supported by the United States government. Women then mobilized under the banner "Neither coup d'état nor violence against women," creating the movement Feminists in Resistance. Since then human rights violations have increased, converting Honduras into one of the most dangerous countries in the world for social activists. The murder of the Lenca indigenous leader, environmentalist activist, and feminist Berta Cáceres in March 2016 was a response to the political alliances between the indigenous and the feminist movements in Honduras. Both movements denounced the complicities among transnational companies such as the International Financial Corporation of the World Bank, the energy development company DESA, and the Honduran government. Berta Cáceres's struggle for the defense of collective rights of indigenous peoples, for women's rights, for the respect of Mother Earth, and against the strategies of transnational capital dispossession became a symbol of the importance of joining the multiple levels of struggle. Her political energy and commitment have been an inspiration all over the continent.

In Mexico the so-called war against narcotics has justified the militarization of the country and the creation of a penal state that has criminalized social movements. Feminicide continues being a national problem at the same time that violence against women has occurred within the framework of the war against drugs. The use of sexual violence as a repressive weapon against organized women reproduces conventional war strategies that have taken on the most violent forms in the context of the "new informal wars." In this context, the election of Donald Trump as president of the United States in November 2016 gives continuity to a wave of right-wing politics on the continent that has created new contexts of vulnerability and violence against women. In contrast to the Argentinian, Brazilian, or Honduran political processes, the election in the United States is a process in which we did not participate but the consequences of which are affecting all women in the Global South in a profound way.

As a Mexican feminist, I share the concern and feeling of vulnerability that all my co-nationals experience on the other side of the border. At the same time, I share the hope and political energy that was evident in the Women's March, the day after the North American businessman occupied the presidency, which shows that women's response has been proportional to the misogyny, racism, and xenophobia promoted by Donald Trump. It was the greatest of mass demonstrations in the recent history of the United States. Almost a million persons marched in the streets of Washington to remind the president that his politics of hate will not be passively accepted. Responding to the call of feminist organizations and women of color, hundreds of thousands of women and men from different regions of the country traveled to the capital of the United States to manifest their rejection of the new government. There were demonstrations in 670 cities along the width and breadth of the country. The call crossed borders, with parallel events taking place in another 70 cities around the world, from Mexico City to Tel Aviv.

Now, in this time of crisis for leftist political parties and the resurgence of new authoritarianisms, civil society is organizing itself, without political affiliation and in many contexts headed by women who are demonstrating the importance of collective mobilization. In the Women's March on Washington we saw a distinct face of the United States. It was a contrast to the feminists' marches of the decades of the sixties and seventies of the twentieth century that were hegemonized by a liberal rights agenda and headed by white middle-class feminists. These mobilizations were characterized by the widening demand of women's issues and by a different kind of leadership. The principles of unity that circulated in the social networks in the declaration of the Women's March in Washington ["Guiding Vision and Definition of Principles"] began with three fundamental demands: gender justice, racial justice, and economic justice.[13]

We now know that this declaration was the result of intense negotiations among diverse women's movements, and that fundamental issues such as the recognition of collective rights for indigenous peoples, a demand of Native American women, were left outside the document. In spite of these important silences, it was evident that we are witnessing the expression of a coalition of feminist and women movements that are broadening the conception of what should be considered "feminist concerns." Kamala Harris, an Afro-Indian US-American senator of California, criticized in her speech the limited perspectives on women's issues, pointing out that issues such as the economy, national security, health, and education are all women's issues that are threatened by the entrepreneurial, privatizing, and militaristic perspectives of the new administration.

The misogyny that characterized the electoral campaign of Donald Trump, including the offensive video in which he literally spoke of how to "grab the pussy" of the women he works with, has no precedent in other electoral processes nor in the worst years of US-American conservatism. On the other hand, the now president announced his intentions to terminate the Planned Parenthood program, criminalize abortion, and incarcerate women who voluntarily interrupt their pregnancy. Added to this violence is the danger of new structural violence against women that threatens the social justice achievements of recent decades. From this perspective, the institutional racism that has made possible police violence toward the Afro-American and Latino communities is a feminist concern. The participation of mothers from the movement Black Lives Matters on the presidium of the march reminds us of this perspective. Women from poor neighborhoods of the United States suffer the police violence that kills and criminalizes their children. The declaration of the march denounces the increase of 700 percent of women incarcerated from 1980 to the present. Donald Trump has announced that he will increase police presence in poor neighborhoods and that he will not permit "abuse against the police." The economic and violent exploitation against undocumented immigrants is also a feminist concern. "No human being is illegal," chanted the participants in the march. The child Sofia Cruz, daughter of undocumented Mexican immigrants, gave a moving speech, which called for struggling for what is just. "Women are the Wall and Trump is going to pay" could be read on some signs in the march, announcing that women are ready to be a wall of contention against Trump's xenophobic discourse declaring that there will be a deportation of three million undocumented.

The academic and activist Angela Davis reminded us that settler colonialism, militarism, and the expansion of the industrial penitentiary complex are also feminist concerns.[14] The participation of petroleum industry businessmen in Trump's cabinet announces new challenges for Native Americans whose lands continue to be colonialized by transnational petroleum companies; such is the case of the Hunkpapa Lakota nation in Standing Rock. The destruction of nature and global warming are also feminists' concerns. Thousands of women have been displaced by natural disasters provoked by climate change or must walk miles to find water because of droughts. The declaration of the Washington march points out: "We believe that the environment and climate must be protected and that our land and its natural resources cannot be exploited for corporate greed or gain—especially at the risk of public safety and health." This feminist agenda, which recognizes the intersection of multiple exclusions that marks women's lives in the United States and in the whole world, has united a multitude of social movements.

These are the mobilizations that allow us to recuperate hope in these times of authoritarianism and violence. They are the Afro-American, Muslim, Native American, Chicana, lesbian, transgender, undocumented workers, university students, and activist women who have become the conscience of the world. They have shown us the importance of constructing political alliances and to go above our differences to place a stop to the politics of violence and death that attempt to force us to return a hundred years in our struggle for social justice.

Photo by Lunan Ji

Toward a New Feminist Politics of Possibility and Solidarity

Zillah Eisenstein

Coming of Age: Zillah's Story

Zillah Eisenstein: Feminism to me was a particular politic and a particular moment. Being brought up in a communist household with deeply antiracist activism, my three sisters and I would spend Saturday mornings picketing Woolworth's and the segregated lunch counters. That is a particular kind of life: Saturdays picketing, and also being very young at that time—I was ten, twelve—and being violated and accosted for being part of the civil rights movement. It made me brave at a very young age, I must say—and the bravery of my parents, who were, particularly my father, clearly Marxist and antiracist. He was tough on us as his daughters. There were times when we would just wish he would let us just do and be. Anyhow, this was at the core of my being and, of course, for my sisters as well. The people who loved us the best and supported us the best were Black, and a lot of the hatred came at us from whites, particularly white Jews who were part of institutionalized synagogues. I should also say we were raised atheist, so that was just part of our identity.

The world in the early to mid-sixties was the height of so much of the civil rights, but then you have the Vietnam War and you have the beginning of different aspects of the women's liberation movement. I started to identify as a feminist, not just an antiracist, and someone who was against war—in this moment it was Vietnam. My older sister, Sarah, was very involved in some of the earliest radical women's groups—socialist, particularly—in Boston. I started to connect with that through her, being somewhat younger and at the fringes of it. But so much of the debate and difficulty that I went through was very intimate in my household, because my father did not see the need for a different feminism from Marxism. So, whereas many people have arguments with their parents, [my argument] was to be able to be a feminist as well as a Marxist and antiracist. That was the beginning. It was at that point that I became very involved in the antiwar movement, but as a feminist, to not be relegated to left politics. So, of course, during the run-up to the 2016 presidential election, it feels like everything I have been doing is saying that progressive politics is not good enough for feminism or antiracism.

Chandra Talpade Mohanty: How similar this moment is to those early years.

ZE: Exactly. I have been brought to advise and discuss with some of the young feminists in the Bernie Sanders campaign. That work is so interesting. The arguments are almost identical. He is not a Marxist, but he is critical of economic inequality and has popularized the term socialism. And his campaign opens this conversation further.

CTM: Bosnia.

Linda E. Carty: Tell us a bit about that moment—in the resistance or forms of resistance to wanting that kind of feminism inside of Marxism. Was there resistance?

ZE: There was enormous resistance, and it was pretty brutal, both intellectually and personally. The earliest intellectual work I did started with my dissertation, and then I did a series of early articles demanding that socialism needed feminism and a discussion of how capitalism needed patriarchy. At that point I was not ready, as a white woman, to theorize racism into that system. That comes later for me, in *The Color of Gender*.[1] But in that early period I was disinvited to many leftist activities, and I was called a revisionist—and, of course, what could be worse? I thought, "Good! We need revision all the time." Then, of course, the way that you are attacked for not being smart enough, all of that comes together. I do think that some of my earliest childhood is what gave me the bravery to say, "I am not stupid. I know what I am doing, and I really want to work with other people who want to do this."

CTM: I am thinking about *Capitalist Patriarchy and the Case for Socialist Feminism*,[2] which was actually a book that traveled all over the world. I remember reading some of that and thinking nobody had been doing this work. We had a tradition of Marxist-feminists in India, but they had not been published in the same way and taking on the same questions as that book, and that book is where the Combahee River Collective is first published.[3] It is so interesting that that was so groundbreaking. And of course a book comes out and you have no clue about the labor and the costs are that are associated with doing stuff like that.

LEC: That is why I asked the question about the resistance, because I remember the antagonism on certain levels to that book in certain circles on the left. It did not deal with, as you said, the race question, because you were not there yet. But they still had incredible resistance, because to insert patriarchy into Marxism is to really challenge them on the woman question.

ZE: Marxists talked about women and women's labor all the time, but not structurally as a system. Here we are still trying to get people to see what "structural" means, and it does not mean what it did thirty years ago. There are new brilliant structures that make it look different and more complicated. Some of the complexity opens up new possibilities for mobilization and camaraderie, as long as we nurture them and try to see the complexity of it.

To give full recognition to the different kinds of feminism, I will share an anecdote. When some of the most brutal attacks were happening about my Marxist feminism, I was asked to participate in a meeting that President Carter was calling to meet with feminists. Bella Abzug at that time was very key in organizing this, and it was for feminists to tell Carter what we wanted—the different kinds of feminism.[4] When she called and asked me to come, I said to her, "Bella, I talk to Marxists about *why* they need to be feminist. I don't know how to talk to liberal feminists about *how* they should become Marxist." I hung up the phone. A group of socialist feminists were having dinner with me. They said, "Zillah, try it!" We sat there and I tried to figure out what could I say. What I said then changed my life. I said, "Okay, you say you want to be equal to men? Which men do you want to be equal to?" That started the dialogue. What was amazing was that it was a lot easier to get feminists to become Marxist than it was to get Marxists to become feminist. That was fully transformative, and that was why the book that came out of that struggle was called *The Radical Future of Liberal Feminism*,[5] which has not happened.

CTM: I went to one such meeting that Valerie Jarrett called for Obama.[6] I remember sitting in that room. There were quite a few women of color in there, but the discourse was very much a liberal feminist discourse. They wanted to talk about what should be the agenda for women's studies and women's rights. It is a neoliberal frame. The level at which I remember being able to get through was when I started talking about truncated citizenship and what citizenship means. It is so interesting—the presidents seem to do this periodically, and it is meaningful only to the extent that you can connect with the other communities or people that are in the room and then figure out what the agenda can be.

LEC: But in the Carter period, they specifically wanted to talk about feminism and some elements of Marxism.

ZE: We were in this particular moment when it looked like Hillary Clinton was probably going to be a presidential candidate and maybe even the president. When Donald Trump was challenging her on her woman card, she said, "I'm in on this." What was she in on? She was in on women's rights as opposed to justice for women. The other point she said was "I'm in for women being treated the same as men." I heard that and I thought, "This is backwards."

LEC: I was thinking with a group of young feminist women of color saying there is no movement that has taken place for this woman. There really is not any kind of movement that has taken place, because what is it that she is fighting for now? What about the questions of social justice? What about the inclusiveness? She wants women to get equal pay for work that men would get the same pay for, but what needs to happen for that to take place? She said nothing about analyzing the economy, what is going to happen in the workplace, what kinds of questions we need to ask. She does not have any movement thinking to go forward into that. It is just discourse.

CTM: Zillah, how have the particular challenges you have faced had a key impact on how you begin to rethink what your goals are? What are the shifts that happen because of these moments and the particular intellectual political challenges that you face?

ZE: At this point that I trust the world to keep me honest and fully involved in trying to find out what an antiracist, anti-imperialist feminism really looks like. That is a big abstract question. What that looks like is when you are asked to actually deal with, let's say, the TRAP [Targeted Regulation of Abortion Providers] laws in the United States, in Alabama and Mississippi, that are making it impossible for poor Black women to get abortions; or you have to rethink what is the difference about abortion today in this country, and how is class redefining it such that so many middle-class women do not have to worry about it because of the morning-after pill, while poor people still do, and there is no middle-class basis for mobilizing around abortion.

Why is it that we are so quiet about reproductive rights in this country as they are completely being challenged? I want to completely support Planned Parenthood, but their politics is still very mainstream and liberal. Not neoliberal, but liberal. So . . . I wonder what is going to happen for those of us who are committed to an anti-imperial framework. What is going to be our responsibility here? To do something and to say something. And then also, what is the responsibility of white women within the different women's movements—because we don't have a unified one—in trying to negotiate an honest coalition that asks more than for me to be an ally, that asks for me to be an active participant in the struggle?

CTM: You have been doing some of this work as a white woman with feminists of color communities, specifically Black women's communities, around many issues—for example, the murder of Black women. Giving some concrete examples would be useful.

LEC: I want to tack on this part: What do you see happening with young feminists to make this movement that you are talking about come about? How is the coalition to happen if in some communities that work is not taking place? What is happening with white feminists to make this movement possible?

ZE: It is a difficult question. I am not sure. I think that the least organized part of feminism in the United States is white women. Of course, that is not really fair. That is putting my blinders in there. For example, there is Planned Parenthood.

CTM: But you are defining an antiracist, anti-imperialist feminism, and you are saying within that the least organized, perhaps, are white women.

ZE: Right. Just like I think that the least articulated ideas of feminism or feminist theory have been [those of] liberal feminism or neoliberal feminism. It is a practice, but it is not a theoretical stand. The most interesting radical work is being done by women of color who are feminists. That is not to exclude the fact that there are anti-antiviolence activists in the United States and globally, but most of them are not white, actually, at this point.

CTM: So now place yourself within that frame, and what is it that compels you to see this because of your history and to actually figure out ways to build a coalition or the solidarities that allow this kind of work? I think that would be really instructive as a pedagogical or strategic practice.

ZE: What I think is really difficult about coalition work right now is that there are a lot of serious fractures within communities, and the way that you find the ability to make coalition is that you need people who voice the need for it. On some level the people who can voice it least well at the moment are white women. Or I think that many of them think that.

CTM: Why?

ZE: Some of it has to do with this idea of ally. In other words, you support but you do not lead. I would agree with that, but at the same time the idea of being enormously invested and involved need not be a position of leadership. These are all very difficult issues that need to be talked about. People need to trust each other enough to work on it. I did some of the work and writing about trying to see Black women, and "say her name," and mobilize around the violence against Black women, and deal with the structure of patriarchy as well as racism, as Kim Crenshaw, originator of the term "intersectionality" does. It becomes difficult for many white women who do not have an articulated stance. Their idea of being involved is to be supportive but not actually to be an activist.

Even in all of the discussion about [the album] *Lemonade* and Beyoncé, there has been a lot of stuff that says, "This is a Black woman's moment. This is about Black women," and as a white woman I think, "Yes, I am ready and willing to love this story and to enlarge my life with it, but don't say that this is just a Black woman's story." Maybe all of us suffer a bit for the narrative in our society of exceptionalism, so we are exceptional as a country and each of us have an exceptional history, which is both true and not.

CTM: Exactly. But also that prevents any kind of critical engagements with other communities. It prevents even criticizing other communities.

LEC: That is true and that is what frustrates us, . . . but a part of this reality is that the feminism that we want has not happened yet, because the breadth of antiracist feminism is not being done in a large enough frame. So I have to constantly use Zillah's work, because you are looking at white feminism to find that it is not there. The coalition you are pointing to feels and seems almost impossible, and that is why *Lemonade* is taking that position, and the discussion around *Lemonade* is going in that direction because "It's a Black women's moment. It's about them. We can't really engage here, or we shouldn't, too much," without recognizing that this is your responsibility, too, because it is inclusive of all of us. What has happened there is more than Black women's story.

ZE: Right, and the "more" has nothing to do with saying less. That is the point. When I wrote *The Color of Gender*, for the first time, as a white woman, I was going to risk everything. I knew I would not do it perfectly, but I had my dad in my heart and brain, and my mother.

The subtitle of the book is *Reimagining Democracy*. You may not remember this, but the end of the book basically says the way that we can maybe come closer to democracy is to imagine a Black woman who is pregnant. Intellectually, the idea was to say that we are all trained to think that the more specific we are, the narrower we are. I argue here that the more specific we are, the more inclusive and the more general we are, because if we can meet the needs of that Black woman, that would exclude no one—even though I thought, "Oh, my god, I'm making her pregnant, this is ridiculous!" But I couldn't do it any better. So I thought, "What the hell, try it!"

The point here was to say that this specific lens excludes no one. So in other words, you could be a white man, and as long as those needs are being met for this Black pregnant woman, nobody is excluded. That is the inclusive moment. I am saying this as a political philosopher. The shit I took for that! But it was really asking for the revision of what people would say. When students in my classroom would say, "I'm not a feminist, because that's too specific; I'm a humanist, because that means I'm talking to everybody." I used to say, "No, be a feminist and you might get to—"

CTM: Talk about what you want.

ZE: And that the whole history of the world has been what? We took the universal right and tried to push everyone in, and now we are still doing that. Which is why I would say, intellectually, liberal democracy does not work, because we will just keep—

CTM: Adding people. "Now we have refugees, and people who have come from this other country."

LEC: We have a big diverse pie, but we have intense oppression that is continuing, because we are still not doing the inclusive work of antiracist feminism. It does not mean to just talk about Black women, but even that is not happening in the white feminist community.

ZE: The other thing is we are so much more a diverse country than we were in the sixties. Black/white just does not do it. I was just thinking, "My god! All of the ways that women of different colors are punished for their 'Becky with the good hair.'" If we could just corral all of us together here! I wish that Black feminism was taken seriously enough to actually be inclusive in this kind of way. Of course, then I am back to "And I am a white woman." The point here is that you have to risk everything, and people almost have to do that simultaneously. I understand that white women have to be willing to really risk right at the get-go, because the assumption is we are not going to.

CTM: Do you see a critical mass of antiracist white feminists doing this work? I see some in movements, but I do not see enough in the academy. I do not see people teaching this. Some of what needs to happen is people have to be teaching it, like you were teaching it. When you were teaching, what kind of community (of white feminists) did you have that you felt were doing what you were doing?

ZE: The fabulousness of the seventies and into the early eighties is that there was a women's movement that could make us all brave. I did not care about what anyone said about me in my institution or in the academy. They did not value my work. It was only many years later when, because of feminists that valued my work, that my discipline came to give me any level of recognition. But now women do not have that source of support outside. I do not think we can be inside without some piece of our bodies outside, and so people have to find that. I do think that people find it, but it is hard to find it for most women. The source of radicalism of feminism came from the university through the mid-eighties, and it does not anymore. I do not want to be saying this and excluding someone who is doing important work because other people are.

The first time I met bell hooks and Angela Davis was at Haverford College, to do a panel called "Racism and the White Women's Movement," and then I continued to know them. Through a good portion of the eighties there was an incredible radical community of feminists of all sorts. It was to the extent that the conferences were even funded through universities and colleges. That is how we did work. Today there is nothing. You go to an individual conference. Barbara Smith and I never lived in the same town. I did not live in the same place as anyone. There was a sense of community and it was much more international. I did a huge amount of work in Canada at that time.

CTM: It was a very different moment. So what is it going to take for us to actually intervene?

LEC: It has to start with more courage. Wouldn't you say that we have to really deconstruct the kind of capitalism that we see starting in the United States? It forces one to do antiracist feminist work, because you see the lack of inclusiveness, the separateness, and the exclusivity that is so destructive. That is what the state supports. Look at the structure of what the state can become in this country after this election. It is a huge step backward. Even if Hillary is elected, it is not going to be as bad as if Trump is elected.

ZE: Depends on what you are looking at. One of the questions is, Could we really mobilize an incredibly progressive antiracist feminist agenda that exposes the white neoliberal feminism of Hillary? Not to see that she does not get elected, but rather to say that these are the demands. You want our vote? This is who we are. Nobody takes women seriously, politically, even in the narrow electoral sense. The question is, How could we possibly do that? Some of the work was begun with the Bernie Sanders campaign. Then maybe it will be time to try to build a coalition between different women-of-color groups here, along with the antiviolence, which already has huge numbers of young Black feminists in it.

Sexual violence is at the core of war, so how can we not make that anti-imperialist at the same time and really see if we couldn't mobilize? That is also where we are going to see the incredible complexity of politics at the moment, because there are many Black feminists right now who are very supportive of Hillary. What I am saying is that I do not see how we can remain silent, because it is going to get hugely messy. Trump has already made this an issue. Feminism, or at least womanhood, is now going to be an issue.

LEC: There are so many levels to this. Part of it has to do with much of the African American history in this country, the civil rights movement, and what the transformations that have taken place have meant for those people; transformations which are incredibly significant, which we must recognize, which we could never forget. But on a certain level when there are critical moments like this frightening moment right now, the narrow frame of elections in this country creates a certain kind of fear that one feels as a Black person that that history is going to be erased. And not just the history being erased but also the people; they are feeling threatened in particular kinds of ways.

The community finds itself embracing and supporting certain things that are retrograde, because they can only imagine what the alternative is. The fear intensifies and you think, "Well, it is so much better than what the alternative looks like." So you hear people— John Lewis—saying, "Well, Bernie Sanders wasn't there in the sixties when we were there," when none of it is true. That is so disturbing, because that is the kind of thing that is preventing the coalition that is necessary on all levels. Of course, we see on the feminist level what is important and how we can do this, but that seems more possible to me than the larger coalition that is necessary.

ZE: That goes back to something I said earlier about the incredible complexity of the system of racism in this country. There is a lot of Black power leading this country. There was a Black president. But the point here is that need to find ways of building a coalition that recognizes the complexity of that community, of the community of Black women, of the community of white women. The point here is that the points of coalition cannot be as though we are each homogenous. I do not think we have developed a coalitional strategy.

CTM: No, partly because the frames that we are using are not the deeply intersectional frames that we need to use. How else do you not homogenize communities? How else do you complicate identity politics but through thinking about the crisscrossing frames that are a part of all our communities, no matter where in the world we come from? You are right that it is not happening in the ways that it should, ways that we want it to happen.

ZE: But I think we are ready. What is it going to take to mobilize the connectivity rather than the differences?

CTM: Or the divisions, more than the differences.

ZE: Right. Even the fact that there is a hierarchy here; there is a power struggle. The complexity right now is that actually there is the new potential for a shared coalition. There are new possibilities. It is part of the success of the oppressive moment that we live in that we are not pushing for those possibilities.

LEC: In the next couple of weeks to a month, it is probably going to come to a crisis, because the Democratic Party will have to think about the part of Bernie Sanders's campaign that they must embrace. He has brought the discussion to a phase they cannot ignore, and I am completely hopeful that is the moment when the insertion of the necessities of the antiracist feminist will happen, depending on whether he takes a position or withdraws, saying, "I can't tell my supporters what to do."

ZE: Given the work I have done supportive of the Bernie Sanders campaign, not as part of it, I think that unless there are articulated antiracist feminist voices that come out, this will not happen. Many women have been very open to making absolutely sure that it is an antiracist agenda, but we did not get most of it in play. So the point here is, it would have to be put in play, and I will be talking to both of you if it looks like there could be something we could do that people have to do wherever we are.

LEC: What do you see as the future of feminism that we have just talked about in this country? In line with what we have discussed and all of the historical moments in that trajectory we went through—which is yours and so much larger, because we have followed your work, and it has been pioneering in so many ways—where is your hope for the future of feminism in this country?

ZE: My hope is for a deeply revolutionary antiracist feminism that embraces the complexity of the new meanings of racism and the new meanings of a misogyny that are no longer homogenous categories. The period of chattel slavery—it was homogenous. It is not homogenous today. Given the different layers of class—and therefore the different experiences of gender and race—it seems to me if we do not come to that complexity, we cannot have a feminism that matters, and for me feminism is the heart of any possibility. I am hopeful that we can really embrace the newest levels of fraction and faction within ourselves. What were some of the most difficult conflicts in the early part of the women's movement? It was not race, not in terms of whiteness at that time. It was the gay/straight split. I remember so many of my friends who were gay and my heterosexual privilege, both having to defend myself and also expose myself. The point here is if we took that today, it is so much more complex. I mean there are multiple choices.

CTM: And multiple privileges.

ZE: Exactly. That was the simplicity of feminism at that time. I argued early on that . . . simplicity is what radical feminism was allowed to declare as a revolutionary critique against patriarchy. If we are going to do our historical analysis, I don't know where we would be without that. History allowed it.

CTM: It is the same as the anticolonial struggle and the fight against slavery. Those were moments when those arguments were key to any form of thinking about freedom or liberation. What does that mean now? What are the core issues, questions, identities, and ways of thinking that need to be rethought for the same kind of passion to happen around freedom?

ZE: This project that you are doing bespeaks the fact that nothing stands still, and feminism is what it is in the moment that is demanding it.

LEC: Well, this moment is demanding it, and it is also demanding a new way of thinking about it. How to get those experiences and those historical moments in the psyche of people now who are antagonistic to those things, and to project it forward. The T-shirts and the audiences that you see at a Trump campaign are vile, yet that is public and acceptable. It is narrow for us to say that the people who are running to be president of this country, that that is "a political kind of thing," or narrow politics. It is scary to people's existence. People are talking about how to migrate if this is going to be the leadership. Where that level of misogyny is acceptable, it is scary, and when it is compounded by race and everything else, you just feel like there is no space in this brand of capitalism for me and what I look like, represent, believe in, or my coalition struggles. No space. It's very threatening. Very, very threatening. Because the reality is that Trump could become president. I know when we think about it, we are thinking, "Hell, no, we're not going to let that happen, but . . ."

CTM: He can become president, but if you think about women who have struggled in resistance in different parts of the world under the most totalitarian and fascist regimes, you also need to pay attention to what are the ways we can be more courageous, brave, creative, and imaginative about the kind of communities we are fighting for. That is the only way we have survived, because if we actually allowed ourselves to think that the state is completely determining of who we are, or the institution we teach at is completely determining it, we would not do any of the work that we did.

Part of it is also what you said earlier. One foot in and one foot out, and being able to create the communities of resistance that can help us imagine and enact—relationally, at least—a different kind of future. To me, what feminism has really radically done is provided different moments and spaces, historically, to rethink and imagine communities on different grounds than the kind of oppressive, privileged, capitalist, sexist, misogynist, racist communities that the nation, for instance, in many places has put in place. So that is really hopeful in some ways.

LEC: It is. There are moments where I feel excited and hopeful—for example, I am thinking of what the next two weeks to a month will be like, what Bernie Sanders can do, can't do, and how many of us are doing all kinds of work outside, that we want to impact that. But there also are moments when I feel, "Damn, this is . . . ," because the courage that we have seen is necessary. The courage that those women in the Global South who have everything to lose—and "everything" is very little—and they come out and they fight; we do not see that courage here.

CTM: They get killed and they get assassinated. How can we not be in the streets? That is where the neoliberal ideology comes in, which tells people that we have it good, no matter what. We still are number one in certain ways, and we do not feel the urgencies—except for those people who live those urgencies. Those are some of the challenges of solidarity that are so hard to think within the culture we live in right now in the United States. See what is happening in India with the actions that students are organizing because the state is so clearly repressive and criminalizing?[7] We know here, after Black Lives Matter and all of the violence against Black women and the deaths of Black women, that the state is a criminal and criminalizing. We know what the state is doing. But are we seeing the kind of large numbers of people out on the streets? We are not.

ZE: On this, I think that if it were possible to get a massive coalition of women's groups out there on a given day, whatever the differences between them, in the same way as the Climate Change March, New

York City, 2014, which was all different groups; it was not unified. We were every different kind of group out there. I am hoping that maybe—

CTM: There will be a call for something like that.

Further Reflections: Imagining a Revolutionary Feminist Politics

ZE: What to do? How to share my life learning's with younger activist scholars? It is to ask for heart, and courage, and continual transformation of each of us, because the world changes around us, and with us, and against us all the time. And try to learn from our mistakes and do not make them again. I always hope and wish for coalition together in new revolutionary solidarity. We must imagine the world and ourselves in new revolutionary ways. Our imaginations allow us to begin the struggle toward liberation. If revolution does not seem possible, it remains impossible. So I am eager to see what newer and younger antiracist/anti-imperial feminists will do.

But it is just days after racist/misogynist/Islamophobic Donald Trump was elected US president. So my questions and concerns are directed especially to white antiracist feminists in the US. I am disheartened that white women voted for Trump. White antiracist feminists must address this dilemma. Despite the misogynist racist campaign of Trump, 53 percent of white women voted for him. We must ask how misogyny, racism, and poverty as well as class privilege nurtured this cross-class racist voting of white women. It remains for young white antiracist feminists to find out how misogyny was used to mobilize a vote that was deeply racist and how racism was also used to mask misogyny. White women, seeing the changing racial makeup of the world's population, were willing to embrace racism for the protection of their white privilege. They appear willing to embrace a misogynist presidency in order to do this. These choices create a formidable challenge to a multiracial feminist agenda. Despite this huge challenge, I remain deeply committed to building new sites for coalition and trust. This work can build an optimism that believes that radical change can happen. We have to be open to this capacity in order to envision and demand it. I am hoping that new ways of building a white antiracist coalition will emerge out of the past half century of antiracist feminist struggle to finally abolish the white privilege that underpins misogyny across the globe.

Regimes of violence and terror across the planet make everything hard. Maybe the excesses of injustice are on "our" side in that they let us see each other with more embrace. The big "we" of us is everywhere and embedded in every struggle: home-care workers' rights, anti–sexual violence campaigns, domestic violence activism, prison and incarceration reform and abolition, reproductive justice work, workers' rights, abortion rights, immigration reform, climate change, anti-fracking, racial justice movements, voting rights, and antiwar activists. The urgency of this moment—post–US presidential election—feels daunting. Right-wing misogynist governments are gaining strongholds from Trump, to Modi,[8] to Putin, and beyond. The planet is melting, more than sixty million refugees are homeless and stateless, the war on Aleppo is devastating, three hundred million children live in compromised air space and suffer asthma and mental deficits, Yazidi women are torn from their homes and raped but still fight back, misogyny and racism have been remobilized in the election of Trump.[9]

To feminists across this planet, especially the young and new white antiracist women, we need you to build coalitions from these ongoing struggles that are deeply committed to abolishing white privilege. Hopefully you can bring today's margins to find and build a new center. I hope you will use an intersectional stance as your building block. See complexity, multiplicity, mutual dependence, marbling, intertwining, overlapping, interconnecting between yourselves and the issues at hand. Singular and exclusionary identities do not help build solidarity. Build solidarities across all boundaries and borders: national, transnational, gendered, raced, sexed, trans, cis, Black, white, and Latina. Look for the similarities across differences. Every problem you embrace should be seen in its multiple and diverse forms.

I caution white antiracist feminists to make sure to take responsibility for our whiteness and its imperial privilege. As a white antiracist feminist living in the heart of empire, I/we must be very careful to never forget this. Imperial feminism remains a problem even though Hillary was not elected. It is a feminism that operates on behalf of US empire building. It has a history of using the Western canon of "women's rights" to justify US wars, most recently in Iraq and Afghanistan. It imposes rather than negotiates. It dominates rather than liberates. It declares itself the exceptional arbiter of women's needs. It operates on behalf of the hierarchies of class across the globe, leaving most women out of the mix.

I will name this dream of mine, along with Angela Davis,[10] an "intersectional, abolitionist feminism." It will coalesce with the Arab Spring, and Occupy Wall Street, and the Black Lives Matter movements. I am reminded of my friend Egyptian feminist Nawal el Saadawi's response to a question she was asked at a teach-in in New York City just after the Egyptian revolution in Tahrir Square.[11] When asked what people in the US could do to support the revolution in Egypt, she said, "Make your own revolution and change your government for us." I am hoping that the newest feminists in the US and across the planet will now finally make the complex abolitionist feminist revolution that we all are waiting for.

Photo by Alexander Warren Phillips

Toward a Politics of Refusal and Hope

Taveeshi Singh

In refusing to noiselessly inhabit unjust and unequal gender and caste hierarchies, I can trace my first feminist acts back to early childhood. That was before my acts of refusal were perceived to be incongruous with my gender, before they became cause for my mother to worry that she had brought into the world a willful,[1] rebellious, and too-independent-for-her/my/our-own-good daughter. The refusals took place within the most political of spaces: home and school—the building blocks of a society, the foundation upon which structures of power are built and injustices carried out. Too often home and education spaces are considered to be "neutral" spaces, where politics do not and should not enter.

The genealogies of scholar-activists in this volume animate the politics of home and education. Their narratives disrupt commonly accepted notions about the kinds of decisions women are expected to make, the kinds of trajectories their lives are expected to take, customary conceptualizations of family and women's work, and the role of imagination in creating a vision for the future. Individually, these narratives inspire and instruct the listener in the multiple possible entries to feminist consciousness and multiple possible engagements with feminist ethics. Taken together, they show that scholarship is not separable from activism, work is not separable from life, and joy is not separable from struggle.

As a young feminist—relatively younger in age than scholar-activists in this volume, as well as young in terms of political actions carried out in the "public" realm—located in the United States and India, trying to find an entry point into the large body of anticapitalist, anti-imperialist, and antiracist feminist work, and trying to understand how to apply my understanding of this body of work as praxis in resisting the nexus between white supremacy, capitalist patriarchy, and Brahmanical patriarchy, I have found it deeply valuable and pleasurable to work with and explore the Feminist Freedom Warriors archive.

I have listened to the narratives unfold as they were being recorded, and again when they were edited and transcribed. Each time I revisit a narrative, I come away with a deeper understanding of the collective genealogies of women's struggles for justice and dignity, not just specific to each scholar-activist, but also, more broadly, in different locations in the Global South and the Global North. Enfolded in these narratives are threads of multiple, interconnected revolutionary histories drawn from the life experiences of women who have struggled together against forces of oppression, even while geographically apart.

In listening closely, over and over again, I hear what it takes on a daily basis to do coalition and resistance work: the emotional and physical labor of organizing actions, participating in movements, building solidarities, and forging epistemic friendships,[2] while negotiating multiple minority identities, day jobs, and natal and chosen families. In these conversations, I hear the things that are rarely discussed in classrooms, books, and articles; the excavation work of writing defining scholar-activist texts; the grit work behind defining scholar-activist actions; the collective work of sustenance that makes it all possible. I hear the stories that don't always find their way to young feminists who draw power, wisdom, and healing from their elders' traditions of feminism—for example, stories about the work of refusal.

FFW narratives show that struggle begins with refusal, and there are many stories of refusal between the covers of this book: the refusal to accept humiliating treatment, the refusal to let marginalized communities be disappeared, the refusal to take shelter in gender/class/racial privilege in exchange for societal protection, the refusal to be complicit with oppressive natal communities, the refusal to vote for a racist-sexist political party, the refusal to limit political actions to the realm of electoral politics, the refusal to accept the left's erasure of gender justice, the refusal to let claims of objectivity devalue feminist activism and scholarship, and the refusal to let profit motives determine the direction, purpose, or audience of one's work.

But if refusal is the first step to resistance, it can also be the thing that keeps struggle alive. The refusal to give up on an antiracist, anti-imperialist, anticapitalist, anti-caste feminist imaginary is the refusal to give up hope for change. In my short time in the United States, I have witnessed young activists prioritizing consistent participation, to whatever extent possible, in local actions to fight for change through nationwide movements such as Black Lives Matter,[3] Standing Rock,[4] the movement for trans rights,[5] and Boycott, Divestment, and Sanctions.[6] In this time I have also witnessed, albeit from a greater distance, students in university campuses across India steadily express their outrage at discriminatory attitudes, laws, and policies.[7] These are people that not only dared to imagine a more just world but also acted on their new imaginary. Their collective energies catalyzed many Indian students in the United States to draw connections between practices of oppression in both countries and apply that knowledge to generating, reviving or participating in practices of resistance in both locations. The flow of practices of resistance from one location to another and the connection between how a feminist imaginary is mobilized into material change on a day-to-day basis are reflected in the scholar-activists' narratives in this book too.

Drawing from these reflections, when I think of the everyday practices that could support me and my peers in sustaining hope for change I think of (1) resisting, together, the pervasive seductions of late capitalism, (2) objecting emphatically to the narratives of white-American/ Brahmanical-Hindu exceptionalism (and similar supremacist formulations in other locations) that are peddled into our homes and schools through channels of corporate media and governance, and (3) seeking out meaningful ways of connecting with communities that have been engaged in struggles for justice longer than some of us have been alive. Refusal, then, is not a state of inaction; it is a state of active, intergenerational resistance across social and geographical locations. For feminist freedom warriors of any generation, in any location, both refusal and collective struggle are ethical imperatives.

I hope these narratives will find their way to young feminists and activists across the world, *especially* first-generation feminist-activists, who recognize in themselves the willfulness to refuse the path of least resistance and seek a history to locate themselves. I also hope parents will read these narratives so that they are encouraged in the knowledge that the next generation of feminist-activists are stepping into a rich tradition of serious social justice work. Finally, I hope listeners and readers will be inspired to return to the narratives for a second, third, or fourth engagement—these many-layered narratives have much to offer for anyone contemplating becoming a feminist freedom warrior.

Chandra Talpade Mohanty and Linda E. Carty; photo by Paula Johnson

Biographies

Linda E. Carty is a Black feminist scholar-activist and educator in the African American studies department at Syracuse University. Linda's activist and research work spans Black labor struggles, migration, and sexuality in Canada, the Caribbean, and the United States. She is author of the articles "A Genealogy of Marxist Feminism in Canada" (2014); "Not a Nanny: A Gendered, Transnational Analysis of Caribbean Domestic Workers in New York City" (2003); and "The Discourse of Empire and the Social Construction of Gender" (2002). Linda is editor of the anthology *And Still We Rise: Feminist Mobilization in Contemporary Canada* (1993). She is coauthor/contributor to *We're Rooted Here: Essays in African Canadian Women's History* (1994) and *Unsettling Relations: The University as a Site of Feminist Struggles* (1991).

Linda coauthored "Mapping Transnational Feminist Engagements: Neoliberalism and the Politics of Solidarity" (2014) with

155

Chandra Talpade Mohanty, and "Solidarity Work in Transnational Feminism: The Question of Class and Location" (2009) with Monisha Das Gupta. She works with UNAIDS-Caribbean; has been a member of the Black Women's Collective, Toronto, and the Caribbean Women's Health Association–Immigrant Services, New York City; and is a founding member of the Democratizing Knowledge Collective (http://democratizingknowledge.syr.edu) at Syracuse University.

Chandra Talpade Mohanty is a feminist scholar-activist and educator in the women's and gender studies department at Syracuse University. Chandra's activism, scholarship, and teaching focus on transnational feminist theory, anticapitalist feminist praxis, antiracist education, and the politics of knowledge. She is author of *Feminism without Borders: Decolonizing Theory, Practicing Solidarity* (2003) and coeditor of *Third World Women and the Politics of Feminism* (1991); *Feminist Genealogies, Colonial Legacies, Democratic Futures* (1997); *Feminism and War: Confronting US Imperialism* (2008); and *Sage Handbook of Identities* (2010).

Chandra is a steering committee member of the Municipal Services Project (municipalservicesproject.org), a transnational research and advocacy group focused on alternatives to privatization in the Global South; a founding member of the Democratizing Knowledge Collective (http://democratizingknowledge.syr.edu) at Syracuse University; and Coordinating Team member of the Future of Minority Studies Research Project (http://fmsproject.cornell.edu). She is series editor of "Comparative Feminist Studies" (Palgrave/Macmillan) and was a member of the Indigenous and Women of Color Solidarity delegation to Palestine in June 2011. Linda and Chandra have a long history of collaboration and are co–principal investigators for the Mellon-funded Democratizing Knowledge Summer Institute's "Just Academic Spaces: Crafting New Publics through Radical Literacies" (2015–2018).

Margo Okazawa-Rey is an activist and educator working on issues of militarism, armed conflict, and violence against women. Margo was a member of the Combahee River Collective and is a founding member of the Afro-Asian Relations Council; East Asia-US Women's Network Against Militarism; the Institute for Multiracial Justice; and the International Network of Women Against Militarism. She has a long-standing relationship with social justice work in South Korea and with the Women's Centre for Legal Aid and Counseling in Palestine.

Margo is coauthor of "A Black Feminist Statement" (1978) with the Combahee River Collective and coeditor of *Activist Scholarship: Antiracism, Feminism, and Social Change* (2009). She also coauthored *Women's Lives: Multicultural Perspectives* (1998) and *Beyond Heroes and Holidays: A Practical Guide to Anti-Racist, Multicultural Curriculum and Staff Development* (1998). Margo is currently Elihu Root Peace Fund Visiting Professor in women's studies at the Fielding Graduate University in Santa Barbara, California. She is also professor emerita at San Francisco State University and has held the Jane Watson Irwin Chair at Hamilton College.

Angela Y. Davis is a longtime revolutionary, activist, organizer, writer, teacher, and scholar dedicated to fighting all forms of oppression in the United States and overseas. She is a founding member of Critical Resistance, a national organization dedicated to the dismantling of the prison industrial complex. Internationally, she is affiliated with Sisters Inside, an abolitionist organization based in Queensland, Australia, that works in solidarity with women in prison.

During the last twenty-five years, Angela has lectured in all of the fifty United States, as well as in Africa, Europe, the Caribbean, and the former Soviet Union. Her articles and essays have appeared in numerous journals and anthologies, and she is the author of nine books, including *Angela Davis: An Autobiography* (2013); *Women, Race, and Class* (1981); *Blues Legacies and Black Feminism: Gertrude "Ma" Rainey, Bessie Smith, and Billie Holiday* (1998); *The Angela Y. Davis Reader* (1998); *Are Prisons Obsolete?* (2003); a new edition of *Narrative of the Life of Frederick Douglass* (2010); and *The Meaning of Freedom* (2011). Angela is currently distinguished professor emerita in the History of Consciousness and feminist studies departments at the University of California, Santa Cruz. In 1994 she received the distinguished honor of an appointment to the University of California Presidential Chair in African American and Feminist Studies.

Himani Bannerji is a sociologist and poet from India based in Canada. She is currently professor of sociology at York University, where she also teaches South Asian colonial and postcolonial literature. Himani's interests include antiracist feminism, Marxism, critical cultural theories, and historical sociology. Her research and writing encompass issues relating to patriarchy and class formation in colonial India and strands of nationalism, cultural identity, and politics in India. She is a founder and life fellow of the School of Women's Studies, Jadavpur University.

Himani has authored several books on India and Canada, including *Inventing Subjects: Studies in Hegemony* (2002); *Patriarchy and Colonialism* (2001); *Demography and Democracy: Essays on Nationalism, Gender, and Ideology* (2011); *The Writing on the Wall: Essays on Culture and Politics* (1993); *Thinking Through: Essays on Feminism, Marxism, and Anti-racism* (1995); and *The Dark Side of the Nation: Essays on Multiculturalism, Nationalism, and Racism* (2000). She has edited, coedited, and contributed to *Returning Gaze: Essays on Gender, Race and Class by Non-white Women* (1993) and *Of Property and Propriety: The Role of Gender and Class in Imperialism and Nationalism* (2001). Himani's poetry has been published in the volume *Doing Time: Poems* (1986), and she translated Bengali poems of Subhash Mukhopadhyay, Manabendra Bandyopadhyay, and Shamsur Rahman in *A Separate Sky* (1982).

Minnie Bruce Pratt is a poet-activist with commitments to organizing around intersecting women's and gender issues, LGBT issues, antiracist work, and anti-imperialist initiatives. She was a member of the editorial collective of *Feminary: A Feminist Journal for the South Emphasizing the Lesbian Vision* for five years and coauthored *Yours in Struggle: Three Perspectives on Anti-Semitism and Racism* (1984).

Minnie Bruce has published six books of poetry: *The Sound of*

One Fork (1981); *We Say We Love Each Other* (1985); *Crime Against Nature* (1989); *Walking Back Up Depot Street* (1999); *The Money Machine* (2010); and *The Dirt She Ate: Selected and New Poems* (2003). Minnie Bruce's poetry has been lauded by the Academy of American Poets, *New York Times*, American Library Association, and Fund for Free Expression. She also authored "Identity: Skin, Blood, Heart" and other autobiographical and political essays included in the volume *Rebellion: Essays 1980-1991* and *S/HE* (1995). Minnie Bruce has co-edited *Feminism and War: Confronting US Imperialism* (2008). She has served as faculty for developing an LGBTQ program at Syracuse University, where she held the position of professor of women's and gender studies and writing and rhetoric.

Amina Mama is a widely traveled Nigerian/British activist, researcher, and scholar who has been actively involved in policy advocacy, community activism, and development consultancy at various times in her career. She is currently director of the Feminist Research Institute at UC Davis. Amina was the first Barbara Lee Distinguished Chair in Women's Leadership at Mills College in Oakland, California. Her research is focused on strengthening activism in African contexts. Amina's research interests include culture and subjectivity, politics and policy, women's movements, and militarism.

From 1999 to 2009 Amina lead the establishment of the African Gender Institute at the University of Cape Town. She is founding editor of *Feminist Africa* and authored the books *Beyond the Masks: Race, Gender, and Subjectivity* (1995) and *Women's Studies and Studies of Women in Africa* (1996). In addition to these works, Amina has coedited "Engendering African Social Sciences" (1997) and several book chapters and journal articles. She also coproduced the documentary film *The Witches of Gambaga* (2010).

Rosalva Aída Hernández Castillo is Professor and Senior Researcher at the Center for Research and Advanced Studies in Social Anthropology (CIESAS) in Mexico City. She was born in Ensenada, Baja California, and she earned her doctorate in anthropology from

Stanford University in 1996. Aída worked as a journalist since she was 18 years old in a Central American Press Agency. Since she was an undergraduate she has combined her academic work with media projects in radio, video and journalism. Her academic work has promoted indigenous and women rights in Latin America. She has done field work in indigenous communities in the Mexican states of Chiapas, Guerrero, Sinaloa, and Morelos, with Guatemalan refugees and with African immigrants in the South of Spain. Aída has published twenty two books and her academic work has been translated to English, French, Portuguese, and Japanese. Her most recent book entitled *Multiple InJusticies: Indigenous Women Law and Political Struggle in Latin America* was published by University of Arizona Press (2016). She is a recipient of the Martin Diskin Oxfam Award for her activist research and of the Simón Bolívar Chair (2013–2014) granted by Cambridge University for her academic work.

Zillah Eisenstein is Distinguished Scholar in Residence at Ithaca College, where she has held the position of professor of politics for thirty-five years. Zillah's writing as a political theorist and activist encompasses diverse yet interconnected issues to do with women's differences and building coalitions across, for example, the Black/white divide in the United States; the struggles of Serb and Muslim women in the war in Bosnia; the relationship between socialists and feminists in union organizing; the struggles against extremist fundamentalisms in Egypt and Afghanistan; the needs of women workers in India; the work conditions of young women in the Foxconn factories in China; and the organizing of migrant women workers in Indonesia.

Zillah has also written extensively on the rise of neoliberalism in the United States and around the world. Through her writing she has recorded the demise of liberal democracy, inquiring in depth into the growth of militarist and imperial globalization. Zillah has most recently authored *The Audacity of Races and Genders: A Personal and Global Story of the Obama Campaign* (2009); *Sexual Decoys, Gender, Race, and War in Imperial Democracy* (2007), *Against Empire* (2007); and *Manmade Breast Cancers* (2001). Zillah currently writes for AlJazeera.com and FeministWire.com.

Taveeshi Singh is a graduate student in the social science program and the department of women's and gender studies at Syracuse Uni-versity. Taveeshi's early training was in psychology and photography. Drawing on these experiences, she has done research, policy advoca-cy and visual media work with nonprofit organizations dedicated to health, education, and food security concerns of marginalized rural and urban communities in India. Taveeshi's doctoral work focuses on intersections of gender, caste, and state. She is inspired by femi-nist genealogies, feminist pedagogies, and visual methods. Taveeshi is co-editor and production manager of the Feminist Freedom War-riors project.

Notes

Margo Okazawa-Rey

1. The Combahee River Collective was formed in 1974 by a group of Black feminists in Boston. In "A Black Feminist Statement" they stated: "We are actively committed to struggling against racial, sexual, heterosexual, and class oppression, and see as our particular task the development of integrated analysis and practice based upon the fact that the major systems of oppression are interlocking." It was first published in *Capitalist Patriarchy and the Case for Socialist Feminism* (1978), a collection of essays anthologized by Zillah Eisenstein. Members of the collective at various points in time included Cessie Alfonso, Cheryl Clarke, Demita Frazier, Gloria Akasha Hull, Eleanor Johnson, Audre Lorde, Chirlane McCray, Margo Okazawa-Rey, Sharon Page Ritchie, Barbara Smith, Beverly Smith, Helen Stewart, and Mercedes Tompkins.
2. The Family Red Apple Boycott was an eight-month-long boycott of a Korean American–owned grocery store in the Flatbush section of New York

City, in response to the store owner's assault of a Haitian woman customer. See Claire Jean Kim, "'No Justice, No Peace!': The Politics of Black-Korean Conflict," *Trotter Review* 7, no. 2, article 5, http://scholarworks.umb.edu /trotter_review/vol7/iss2/5.

3. Fifteen-year-old LaTasha Harlins was shot in the back of the head by a Korean American store owner in 1991. See Ayofemi Kirby, "Why We Must Remember the Life of LaTasha Harlins and #SayHerName," Medium.com, https://medium.com/@ayofemi/latasha-harlins-made-in -america-and-murdered-over-o-j-the-juice-not-the-man-sayhername -dbc82a7fa022.

4. Gwyn Kirk is, in her own words, "a scholar-activist concerned with gender-based, racial, and environmental justice in the service of genuine security and a sustainable world." See her biography at http://gwynkirk .com/about/biography.

5. See Gwyn Kirk and Margo Okazawa-Rey, "Making Connections: Building an East Asia–U.S. Women's Network against U.S. Militarism," in *The Women and War Reader*, ed. Lois Ann Lorentzen and Jennifer Turpin, 308–322 (New York: New York University Press, 1998).

6. Malathi de Alwis is a scholar and activist concerned with issues of gender, nationalism, militarism, and resistance. She is Senior Research Fellow at the International Center for Ethnic Studies in Sri Lanka. See her biography at http://mdealwis.squarespace.com.

7. Maha Abu-Dayyeh (1951–2015) was a Palestinian feminist, visionary leader, and cofounder and director of the Women's Centre for Legal Aid and Counselling (WCLAC) in Jerusalem. Faiha Abdulhadi, "Maha Abu-Dayyeh: A Life of Dedication," *The Feminist Wire*, February 17, 2015, http://www.thefeministwire.com/2015/02/maha-abu-dayyeh.

8. Cynthia Cockburn is, in her own words, "a feminist researcher and writer working at the intersection of gender studies and peace/conflict studies." She is a visiting professor in the Department of Sociology at City University of London and an honorary professor in the Centre for the Study of Women and Gender, University of Warwick. See her biography at http://www.cynthiacockburn.org/about.html.

9. Established in 1991, "The Women's Centre for Legal Aid and Counselling (WCLAC) is an independent Palestinian, not-for-profit, non-governmental organisation that seeks to develop a democratic Palestinian society based on the principles of gender equality and social justice. By forging a feminist vision based on equality and social justice, WCLAC has played a prominent role in addressing gender-based violence in Palestinian society in both private and public spheres." See http://www.wclac.org.

10. See Gwyn Kirk and Margo Okazawa-Rey, *Women's Lives: Multicultural*

Perspectives (New York: McGraw Hill, 2010).

11. Chandra Talpade Mohanty, "Cartographies of Struggle: Third World Women and the Politics of Feminism," in *Third World Women and the Politics of Feminism*, ed. Chandra Talpade Mohanty, Ann Russo, and Lourdes Torres, 1–50 (Bloomington: Indiana University Press, 1991).

12. Bernice Johnson Reagon, "Ella's Song." Bernice Johnson Reagon is a musician-producer, scholar-activist, and composer-commentator whose singing, teaching and activism has been dedicated to "speaking out against racism and organized inequities of all kinds." See her biography at http://www.bernicejohnsonreagon.com/about.

13. Amnesty International, "'We Are at Breaking Point'": Rohingya: Persecuted in Myanmar, Neglected in Bangladesh," Amnesty International Report, December 19, 2016, https://www.amnestyusa.org/files/amnesty_myanmar_bangladesh_report.pdf.

14. Septima Poinsette Clark (1898–1987) was an educator and civil rights activist. She came to be known as the "Mother of the [Civil Rights] Movement." See her biography by Marian Wright Edelman, "Honoring Septima Clark," *Huffington Post*, February 28, 2014, http://www.huffingtonpost.com/marian-wright-edelman/honoring-septima-clark_b_4876882.html.

15. Alan Rosenberg, *Echoes from the Holocaust: Philosophical Reflections on a Dark Time* (Philadelphia: Temple University Press, 2009), 382.

16. Anne Braden (1924–2006) was a journalist, civil rights activist, and educator. Her work emphasized the responsibility of whites in combating racism. Anne taught social justice history at Northern Kentucky University and at the University of Louisville. See her biography at http://louisville.edu/braden/about/who-was-anne-braden.

17. On the website for her book *The Next American Revolution: Sustainable Activism for the Twenty-First Century*, Grace Lee Boggs (1915–2015) is described as "an activist, writer, and speaker whose seven decades of political involvement encompass the major US social movements of the past one hundred years. A daughter of Chinese immigrants, Grace received her B.A. from Barnard College (1935) and her Ph.D. in philosophy from Bryn Mawr College (1940). She developed a twenty-year political relationship with the Black Marxist, C.L.R. James, followed by extensive Civil Rights and Black Power Movement activism in Detroit in partnership with husband and Black autoworker, James Boggs (1919–1993)." See her biography at http://gracleeboggs.com/about.

Angela Y. Davis

1.   Angela Davis, *Women, Race, and Class* (New York: Random House, 1981).
2.   Gloria Anzaldúa and Cherríe Moraga, eds., *This Bridge Called My Back: Writings by Radical Women of Color* (Watertown, MA: Persephone Books, 1981).
3.   bell hooks, *Ain't I a Woman: Black Women and Feminism* (Boston: South End Press, 1982).
4.   Michele Wallace, *Black Macho and the Myth of the Superwoman* (New York: Dial Press, 1979).
5.   Gloria Joseph and Jill Lewis, *Common Differences: Conflicts in Black and White Feminist Perspectives* (Boston: South End Press, 1981).
6.   The Common Differences Conference Committee, facilitated by Chandra Talpade Mohanty and Ann Russo, organized an international women's conference on feminist perspectives from the Global North and South at the University of Illinois–Urbana Champaign in 1983. See Katherine Haley, "Common Differences," *Syracuse University News: Arts & Culture*, October 17, 2013, https://news.syr.edu/2013/10/common-differences-50720.
7.   The Women Against Racism Committee organized a four-day national conference called "Parallels and Intersections" at the University of Iowa in 1989. The conference had no registration fees and was attended by over fifteen hundred people.
8.   Cherríe Moraga is a Chicana playwright, poet, and scholar-activist. She is coeditor (with the late Gloria Anzaldúa) of *This Bridge Called My Back*. See her biography at http://cherriemoraga.com/index.php/about-cherrie-moraga-1.
9.   Gloria E. Anzaldúa (1942–2004) was a Chicana poet, writer, and scholar activist. She is the author and coeditor of several groundbreaking works, including *Borderlands/La Frontera: The New Mestiza* (San Francisco: Spinsters/Aunt Lute, 1987) and *This Bridge Called My Back*.
10. bell hooks is described by the bell hooks Institute as a "feminist theorist, cultural critic, artist, and writer" whose "writings cover topics of gender, race, class, spirituality, teaching, and the significance of media in contemporary culture." She is Distinguished Professor in Residence in Appalachian Studies at the Loyal Jones Appalachian Center at Berea College, Kentucky. See her biography at http://www.bellhooksinstitute.com/about.
11. National Women's Studies Association, http://www.nwsa.org.
12. Angela Davis, *Blues Legacies and Black Feminism: Gertrude "Ma" Rainey, Bessie Smith, and Billie Holiday* (New York: Vintage Press, 1999).
13. See Zillah Eisenstein, ed., *Capitalist Patriarchy and the Case for Socialist Feminism* (New York: Monthly Review Press, 1978).
14. Friedrich Engels, *Origin of the Family, Private Property, and the State* (New York: Pathfinder Press, 1972).

15. Francis Beal, "Double Jeopardy: To Be Black and Female," pamphlet published by Third World Women's Alliance, 1969.

16. Activist Scholar Barbara Smith describes the inception of Kitchen Table: Women of Color Press as follows:

> Starting a press for women of color in 1980 may have defied logic, but it was one of those acts of courage that characterize Third World women's lives. In October 1980, Audre Lorde said to me during a phone conversation, "We really need to do something about publishing." I enthusiastically agreed and got together a group of interested women to meet in Boston on Halloween weekend, when Audre and other women from New York were in town to do a Black women's poetry reading. It was at that meeting that Kitchen Table: Women of Color Press was born. We did not arrive at a name or announce our existence until a year later, but at that initial meeting we did decide to publish all women of color, although there were only women of African American and African Caribbean descent in the room. This was one of our bravest steps; most people of color have chosen to work in their separate groups when they do media or other projects. We were saying that as women, feminists, and lesbians of color we had experiences and work to do in common, although we also had our differences. A year later we were officially founded. We chose our name because the kitchen is the center of the home, the place where women in particular work and communicate with each other. We also wanted to convey the fact that we are a kitchen table, grass roots operation, begun and kept alive by women who cannot rely on inheritances or other benefits of class privilege to do the work we need to do.

Barbara Smith, "A Press of Our Own Kitchen Table: Women of Color Press," *Frontiers: A Journal of Women Studies* 10, no. 3, *Women and Words* (1989): 11–13.

17. Angela Davis, "Violence against Women and the Ongoing Challenge to Racism" (New York: Kitchen Table: Women of Color Press, 1985).

18. CeCe McDonald is a Black, trans feminine, prison-abolition activist. CeCe, along with Joshua Allen, also a Black, trans feminine activist, organize for intersectional racial and gender justice through their #BlackExcellenceTour. See Cherise Morris and Rheem Brooks, "Interview with Joshua Allen: Bending towards Freedom: Queer Abolitionist Histories & Black Femmehood," *Bluestockings Magazine*, March 24, 2016, http://bluestockingsmag .com/2016/03/24/bending-towards-freedom-on-queer-abolitionist -histories-black-femmehood.

19. Chandra Talpade Mohanty, "Cartographies of Struggle: Third World Women and the Politics of Feminism," in *Third World Women and the Politics of Feminism*, ed. Chandra Talpade Mohanty, Ann Russo, and Lourdes Torres, 1–50 (Bloomington: Indiana University Press, 1991).

20. Barbara Ransby is, in her own words, "a historian, writer, and longtime activist. She is a Distinguished Professor of African American Studies, Gender and Women's Studies, and History at the University of Illinois at

Chicago, where she directs the campus-wide Social Justice Initiative." She is author of *Ella Baker and the Black Freedom Movement: A Radical Democratic Vision* (Chapel Hill: University of North Carolina Press, 2005) and "a founder of Ella's Daughters, a network of women working in Ella Baker's tradition." See her biography at http://barbararansby.com/about-2. Barbara Ransby spoke with Chandra Talpade Mohanty and Linda Carty for the Feminist Freedom Warriors project on April 8, 2015, in Ithaca, New York. http://feministfreedomwarriors.org/watchvideo.php?firstname =Barbara&lastname=Ransby.

Himani Bannerji

1. See Vijay Prashad, "The Origins of India's Maoist Rebellion," interview, April 7, 2010, http://uprisingradio.org/home/2010/04/07/the-origins-of -indias-maoist-rebellion; and Arundhati Roy, "Walking with the Comrades," *Outlook India*, March 29, 2010, http://www.outlookindia.com/magazine /story/walking-with-the-comrades/264738.
2. Mahasweta Devi (1926–2016) was a Bengali writer and activist who was involved with organizing efforts of the rural dispossessed and Adivasi communities in India. See Kaushik Swaminathan, "Mahasweta Devi, Bengali Writer and Activist Who Fought Injustice, Dies at 90," *New York Times*, August 2, 2016, https://www.nytimes.com/2016/08/03/books /mahasweta-devi-bengali-writer-and-activist-who-fought-injustice -dies-at-90.html.
3. Urvashi Butalia, *The Other Side of Silence: Voices from the Partition of India* (1998; Durham, NC: Duke University Press, 2000).
4. Jasodhara Bagchi and Subhoranjan Dasgupta, eds., *From Trauma to Triumph: Gender and Partition in Eastern India* (Kolkata, India: Stree, 2003).
5. Radha Kumar, *The History of Doing: An Illustrated Account of Movements for Women's Rights and Feminism in India, 1800–1990* (New Delhi: Kali for Women, 1993). Feminist scholar and policy analyst Radha Kumar is chair of the United Nations University (UNU) Council and director general of the Delhi Policy Group. Radha's work is concerned with issues of peace and security and the women's movement in India. She was previously director of the Nelson Mandela Centre for Peace and Conflict Resolution at Jamia Milia Islamia, Senior Fellow at the Council on Foreign Relations in New York, and director of its project on Ethnic Conflicts and Peace Processes.
6. Mary Wollstonecraft (1759–1797) was a political and moral philosopher whose work emphasized the liberation and education of women. See Janet Todd, "Mary Wollstonecraft: A 'Speculative and Dissenting Spirit,'" BBC

History, February 17, 2011, http://www.bbc.co.uk/history/british/empire
_seapower/wollstonecraft_01.shtml.

7. *Meghe Dhaka Tara* [*The Cloud-Capped Star*], dir. Ritwik Ghatak, Chi-trakalpa, 1960.

8. Sheila Rowbotham, *Woman's Consciousness, Man's World* (New York: Penguin Books, 1973). Rowbotham is a socialist feminist historian and author and a professor at the University of Manchester. See her biography at http://www.manchester.ac.uk/research/Sheila.rowbotham.

9. Germaine Greer, *The Female Eunuch* (New York: HarperCollins, 1970). Greer is a feminist writer who was a prominent figure in the second-wave feminist movement. She has taught English literature at the University of Warwick and Cambridge University.

10. See chapter 2, "Troubling Explanatory Frameworks: Feminist Praxis across Generations."

11. Betty Friedan, *The Feminine Mystique* (New York: W. W. Norton, 1963). Betty Friedan (1921–2006) was a writer and a prominent figure in the second-wave feminist movement in the United States. See Joanne Boucher, "Betty Friedan and the Radical Past of Liberal Feminism," *New Politics* 9, no. 3 (new series), whole no. 35 (Summer 2003), http://nova.wpunj.edu /newpolitics/issue35/boucher35.htm.

12. See Paul Weinberg, "The Praxis Affair: There's a reason we put limits on spying within Canada," *The Monitor*, March 1, 2015, https://www .policyalternatives.ca/publications/monitor/praxis-affair.

13. Kate Millett, *Sexual Politics* (New York: Doubleday, 1970). Millett (1934–2017) was a writer, artist, feminist, and human rights advocate. She was a prominent figure in the second-wave women's movement in the United States. See her biography at http://www.katemillett.com /KateMillett/Bio_2.html.

14. The Black Education Project was founded in the late 1960s by activist Marlene Green in response to Black parents' concerns about access to education, dropout rates, and racism in schools, policing and in the workplace. See http://www.ryerson.ca/akua-benjamin-project/who-are-we -celebrating/marlene-green.

15. Dionne Brand, *Primitive Offensive* (Stratford, ON: Williams-Wallace, 1982); Dionne Brand, *Fore Day Morning* (Toronto: Khoisan Artists, 1978). Brand is a renowned poet, novelist, educator, and activist. Her work explores themes of gender, race, sexuality, and national and cultural history. See her biography at http://canpoetry.library.utoronto.ca/brand.

16. Lillian Allen, *Rhythm an' Hard Times* (Toronto: Domestic Bliss, 1982). Allen is, in her own words, "a creative writing professor at the Ontario College of Art and Design University in Toronto, Canada. Allen emerged

from the grass roots in the seventies to become a leading influential figure on the Canadian cultural landscape." Allen, a renowned poet, specializes in the writing and performing of dub poetry. See her biography at http://www.lillianallen.ca/about-lillian-allen.

17. Himani Bannerji, *A Separate Sky* (Toronto: Domestic Bliss, 1982).

18. Sister Vision: Black Women and Women of Colour Press was founded in 1984. It is the first press for Black women and women of color in Canada. Sister Vision was cofounded by Makeda Silvera and Stephanie Martin. See http://www.collectionscanada.gc.ca/women/030001-1212-e.html.

19. "Lee Maracle is a Sto:Loh nation grandmother of four, mother of four who was born in North Vancouver, BC. . . . She currently is Mentor for Aboriginal Students at University of Toronto where she also is a teacher and also the Traditional Cultural Director for the Indigenous Theatre School, where she is a part-time cultural instructor." http://indigenousstudies.utoronto.ca/person/lee-maracle.

20. Roxana Ng (1951–2013) was an educator and activist whose research was concerned with the experiences of immigrant women in Canada, with a focus on institutional ethnography, embodied learning, and the labor market. She was professor of Adult Education and Community Development at the Ontario Institute for Studies in Education (OISE) at the University of Toronto, where she was also the director of the Center for Women's Studies in Education.

21. Sherene Razack is a scholar-activist whose research and teaching is concerned with issues of gender and race in the law. She is professor emerita in the Department of Social Justice Education at the University of Toronto.

22. Linda Carty and Dionne Brand, "'Visible Minority Women': A Creation of the Canadian State," in *Returning the Gaze: Essays on Racism, Feminism, and Politics*, ed. Himani Bannerji (Toronto: Sister Vision Press, 1993).

23. Himani Bannerji, ed., *Returning the Gaze: Essays on Racism, Feminism, and Politics* (Toronto: Sister Vision, 1993)

24. Johanna Stuckey is currently professor emerita of religious studies and women's studies at York University in Toronto, Canada. She has taught courses on goddesses and goddess worship in the ancient eastern Mediterranean and on female spirituality. She has published books on women's spirituality and articles on various goddesses.

25. Patricia Mills is professor emerita of political science at the University of Massachusetts at Amherst.

26. Jasodhara Bagchi (1937–2015) was a prominent Indian feminist critic and women's rights activist. She was chairperson of the West Bengal Commission for Women and founder-director of the School of Women's Studies at

Jadavpur University. See the tribute to Jasodhara Bagchi by scholar-activist and literary translator Sarmistha Dutta Gupta at http://www .gokhalecollegekolkata.edu.in/alumni/Tribute-ProfJasodharaBagchi.pdf.

27. Himani Bannerji, *Inventing Subjects: Studies in Hegemony, Patriarchy, and Colonialism* (London: Anthem South Asian Studies, 2001); Jasodhara Bagchi, *Interrogating Motherhood* (Thousand Oaks, CA: Sage Publications, 2017).

28. Kavita Panjabi is a professor in the Department of Comparative Literature at Jadavpur University. She is also an activist in the Indian women's movement and in the Pakistan-India Peoples' Forum for Peace and Democracy. In 2005 she was Senior Fellow in the Future of Minority Studies (FMS) Research Project at Cornell University.

29. Ernesto Laclau and Chantal Mouffe, *Hegemony and Socialist Strategy: Towards a Radical Democratic Politics* (London: Verso, 1985).

30. *Life and Debt*, dir. Stephanie Black, Tuff Gong Pictures, 2001. http://www.lifeanddebt.org.

31. Rosa Luxemburg (1871–1919) was a socialist revolutionary agitator, writer, theorist, and antiwar activist. See Sheila Rowbotham, "The Revolutionary Rosa Luxemburg," *Guardian*, March 4, 2011, https://www.theguardian .com/books/2011/mar/05/rosa-luxemburg-writer-activist-letters.

Minnie Bruce Pratt

1. Started in 1988, Creating Change is an annual organizing event of the National Conference for LGBT Equality. See http://www.thetaskforce .org/creating-change.

2. Jewelle Gomez is a writer and activist and the author of the novel *The Gilda Stories* from Firebrand Books (1991). She is the former director of the literature program at the New York State Council on the Arts and the director of cultural equity grants for the San Francisco Arts Commission. She is currently the director of grants and community initiatives for Horizon and the president of the San Francisco Library Commission. See her biography at http://www.jewellegomez.com/bio.html.

3. Alabama governor George Wallace's symbolic attempt to stop the desegregation of schools, whereby he stood at the door of Foster Auditorium at the University of Alabama to try to block the entry of Black students, came to be known as the Stand in the Schoolhouse Door.

4. The Children's March was also known as the Children's Crusade, in which more than a thousand African American students marched in downtown Birmingham in support of the 1963 campaign to desegregate Birmingham, Alabama.

5. The Student Nonviolent Coordinating Committee (SNCC) made hugely significant contributions to the civil rights movement through its field-work, including organizing voter registration drives in the South. The committee was formed at a student meeting organized by Ella Baker at Shaw University, in Durham, North Carolina, in April 1960.

6. Minnie Bruce Pratt, "Identity: Skin, Blood, Heart," in *Yours in Struggle: Three Feminist Perspectives on Anti-Semitism and Racism*, by Elly Bulkin, Minnie Bruce Pratt, and Barbara Smith (Brooklyn, NY: Long Haul Press, 1984).

7. Chandra Talpade Mohanty and Biddy Martin, "What's Home Got to Do with It?," in *Feminism without Borders: Decolonizing Theory, Practicing Solidarity* (Durham, NC: Duke University Press, 2003), 85–105.

8. Chandra Talpade Mohanty, "Under Western Eyes: Feminist Scholarship and Colonial Discourses," in *Feminism without Borders*, 17–42.

9. *Workers World* newspaper has been published by the Workers World Party (WWP) since 1959.

10. Minnie Bruce Pratt, "When I Say 'Steal,' Who Do You Think Of?," part 3, *Southern Spaces*, 2004, https://southernspaces.org/content/transcript -when-i-say-steal-who-do-you-think-part-three.

11. THE General Body is a coalition of students, faculty, and staff at Syracuse University that has been organizing actions for transparency, heterogeneity, and equality—values represented in the acronym "THE"—on campus and community-related issues since 2014. See https://thegeneralbody.org/about.

12. The advocacy group "Peoples Power Assemblies [PPA] organizes to em-power workers & oppressed people to demand jobs, education & healthcare while fighting against racism, sexism & LGBT bigotry." http://peoplespowerassemblies.org/about-us.

13. The Women's Fightback Network is active in fighting for women's' rights and against racism, sexism, anti-LGBTQ bigotry, poverty, and war. See http://www.womensfightback.org.

14. For poetry by Minnie Bruce Pratt, see http://www.mbpratt.org.

15. Leslie Feinberg was a transgender warrior, grassroots activist, Marxist historian, journalist and revolutionary communist. Ze "came of age as a young butch lesbian in the factories and gay bars of Buffalo, N.Y. in the 1960s. . . . Ze is known in the lesbian, gay, bisexual and transgender move-ments in the U.S. and countries around the world. . . . As a trade unionist, anti-racist and socialist, Feinberg also organize[d] to build strong bonds of unity between these struggles and those of movements in defense of oppressed nationalities, women, disabled, and the working-class movement as a whole. Feinberg . . . worked for more than three decades in defense of the sovereignty, self-determination and treaty rights of Native nations and for freedom of political prisoners in the U.S. [Ze was] an internationalist

and [was] part of the anti-Pentagon movement since the U.S. war against Vietnam." See Leslie's biography at http://www.transgenderwarrior.org /about.html.

Amina Mama

1. Women in Nigeria (WIN) was established in 1983 following the First Annual Women in Nigeria Conference, held in 1982. For a discussion of WIN in the context of the Women's Movement in Nigeria, see Altine Mohammed and Bene Madunagu, "WIN: A Militant Approach to the Mobilisation of Women," *Review of African Political Economy* 37 (1986): 103–105; Bene Madunagu, "The Nigerian Feminist Movement: Lessons from 'Women in Nigeria,' WIN," *Review of African Political Economy* 35, no. 118 (2008): 666–72.

2. The Brixton Black Women's Group (BBWG) was a women's collective formed in 1970 in South London by women who were involved in the British Black Power movement and the British Black Panther Party. For a discussion of BBWG's aims, constitutions, and political commitments, see Tracy Fisher, "Transnational Black Diaspora Feminisms," in *What's Left of Blackness: Feminisms, Transracial Solidarities, and the Politics of Belonging in Britain* (New York: Palgrave Macmillan, 2012), 65–91.

3. Claudia Jones (1915–1964) was an antiracist feminist activist and journalist. In 1951 she was found guilty by the US government of being a communist and deported to London, where she founded Britain's first Black newspaper, the *West Indian Gazette*, in 1958 and continued to fight racism. For an introduction to Claudia Jones and her writing, see Claudia Jones, "An End to the Neglect of the Problems of the Negro Woman," in *Words of Fire: An Anthology of African-American Feminist Thought*, ed. Beverly Guy-Sheftall, 107–124 (New York: New Press, 1995).

4. Jacqueline Creft (1947–1983) was one of the leaders of the revolutionary New Jewel movement in Grenada, which became independent from the United Kingdom in 1974. She was minister of education in the Popular Revolutionary Government of Granada from 1979 to 1983. Jacqueline was executed with Maurice Bishop, prime minister of Grenada, in October 1983 by troops under the command of General Hudson Austin, who declared himself head of the government. Shortly after the execution, the United States led a military invasion of Grenada. For more about the Grenadian revolution, see http://www.thegrenadarevolutiononline.com.

5. Structural Adjustment Programs were the now discredited austerity programs through which international financial institutions imposed "free"

market policies on indebted nations. They included divestment of the public sector, the imposition of fees and tariffs for public services, and created widespread poverty.

6. Referring to the Babangida coup in 1985 and the Abacha coup in 1993.

7. Pregaluxmi (Pregs) Govender is an antiracist feminist activist, writer, and former member of Parliament of the African National Congress. Since 1974, when she served in the struggle against apartheid, Pregs has been committed to "the interrelated struggles to end racism, classism, and sexist oppression" in South Africa. See her biography at http://www .africanfeministforum.com/pregaluxmi-pregs-govender.

8. The African Gender Institute at the University of Cape Town is a teaching, learning, and research institute that focuses on issues of gender justice, sexuality, and human rights on the African continent. The AGI was founded on feminist philosophy and practice in 1996 and emphasizes collaborative research projects that connect theory, practice, and activism. See the AGI website at http://agi.ac.za.

9. Here I am using the word "borders," in the expanded way that Chandra does in *Feminism beyond Borders*, to include institutional, disciplinary, and geopolitical, as well as the political demographics of gender, sexuality, religion, ethnicity, and the like.

10. The Democratizing Knowledge (DK) Project: Developing Literacies, Building Communities, Seeding Change, launched in 2009, was developed by a group of critical interdisciplinary scholars "with the primary purpose of confronting white privilege, hegemonic masculinity, heteronormativity, and colonial heritages." It aims to construct "ways of 'democratizing knowledge,' revitalizing and transforming the reach of these knowledges to address difference, identity, equality, justice, citizenship, and democracy and making these knowledges more visible, more sustainable, and more institutionally public on the campus and beyond." See http://democratizingknowledge.syr.edu.

11. Women leaders in development NGOs in Kenya and South Africa estimate that women hold only 15–20 percent of director positions there, and the figure for the United States is even lower at 12–14 percent. In the UK, Oxfam International is the only mainstream NGO headed by a woman—Ugandan feminist Winnie Byanyima, who began her NGO career by founding AC-FODE (Action for Development) in Uganda.

12. See Angelika Arutyunova and Cindy Clark, "Watering the Leaves, Starving the Roots: The Status of Financing for Women's Rights Organizing and Gender Equality," Association for Women's Rights in Development (AWID) (2013), https://www.awid.org/sites/default/files/atoms/files /WTL_Starving_Roots.pdf.

13. See Ama Marston, "Women in Leadership: 'It's not going to work the way

we're doing it,'" *Guardian*, August 1, 2013, https://www.theguardian.com /global-development-professionals-network/2013/aug/01/women-in -leadership-international-ngos.

14. Memorable examples include the "miniskirt" marches that have taken place periodically in Uganda and Zimbabwe to resist efforts to impose restrictions on women's dress; the Ghanaian women's street protests over government inaction over serial murders of women between 1997 and 2000; the antiwar sit-ins that took place in Liberia (2003); and protests over the invasion of oil rigs off the coast of Nigeria by hundreds of women in canoes (2003).

Aída Hernandez-Castillo

1. Aída analyzes this and other activist research experiences in her book *Multiple InJustices: Indigenous Women, Law and Political Struggle* (Tucson: University of Arizona Press, 2016).

2. In 2001 the people of Atenco came together in what came to be known as the San Salvador Atenco Farmers' movement and brought to an end the construction of a new airport in Mexico City that was being built on annexed Atenco farmland. For a feminist analysis of this event, see Rosalva Aída Hernández Castillo, "State Violence and Gender in San Salvador Atenco," in *Chicana/Latina Studies* 6, no. 2 (2007): 118–29.

3. A documentary film by the same name about indigenous women in prison in Mexico was made during Aída's workshop "Life Stories" in the Atlacholoaya Morelos prison between 2008 and 2009. To download the documentary film and books written and edited by the inmates, see http://www.rosalvaaidahernandez.com/?page_id=42.

4. See Rosalva Aída Hernández Castillo, "Social Justice and Feminist Activism: Writing as an Instrument of Collective Reflection in Prison Spaces," *Social Justice* 42, nos. 3-4 (2015): 155–69.

5. Red de Feminismos Descoloniales en México (Decolonial Feminist Network in Mexico) is a self-convocated network that is committed to a decolonizing feminist epistemology and "weaves criticism between academia and political mobilization." See https://feminismosdescoloniales .wordpress.com/about.

6. To access the articles Aída has written for *La Jornada*, see http://www .rosalvaaidahernandez.com/?page_id=150.

7. Luchadoras is a multidisciplinary feminist collective of women media producers based in Mexico City. The Luchadoras Collective advocates for women's rights and social justice. They launched the online feminist TV show

Luchadoras in 2012 on RompevientoTV, through which they share stories of inspirational women as drivers of change. See http://www.luchadoras.org.

8. On September 26, 2014, forty-three undergraduate students from Escuela Normal Rural (Rural Teachers College) Raúl Isidro Burgos, in Ayotzinapa, known for its history of activism, were disappeared in the town of Iguala by the Mexican police force. The students had plans to travel to Mexico City to attend a march commemorating the anniversary of the 1968 Tlatelolco massacre. For an analysis of this event and of the responsibility of the state, see https://lasa.international.pitt.edu/forum/files/vol46 -issue1/Debates-11.pdf.

9. Audre Lorde (1934–1992) was, in her own words, "a Black, lesbian, mother, warrior, poet." Audre's activism and writing underscored the importance of the struggle for justice for oppressed peoples and of building coalitions across differences of race, gender, sexual orientation, class, age, and ability. Audre passed away on November 17, 1992. For her biography https://alp .org/about/audre.

10. I used the term "commons" taken from political economy to refer to the natural, social and cultural resources that are accessible to all the society. See Chet *Revitalizing the Commons: Cultural and Educational Sites of Resistance and Affirmation*"http://www .universidadepopular.org/site/pages/en/about-upms/what-is-upms.php.

11. "The Popular University of Social Movements or Universidade Popular dos Movimentos Sociais (UPMS) was created at the 2003 World Social Forum (WSF)—a space for meetings and exchanges among social movements from different parts of the world . . . as a means for linking diverse forms of knowledge [and] strengthening new forms of resistance" "for activists and leaders of social movements and members of non-governmental organizations, as well as social scientists, researchers and artists committed to progressive social change." See http://www.universidadepopular.org/site /pages/en/about-upms/what-is-upms.php.

12. "Boaventura de Sousa Santos is Professor of Sociology, University of Coimbra (Portugal), and Distinguished Legal Scholar at the University of Wisconsin–Madison. . . . He is director of the Center for Social Studies at the University of Coimbra and has written and published widely on the issues of globalization, sociology of law and the state, epistemology, social movements and the World Social Forum." See his biography at http://www.boaventuradesousasantos.pt/pages/en/homepage.php.

13. See "Guiding Vision and Definition of Principles," Womens March, https://www.womensmarch.com/principles.

14. See chapter 2, "Troubling Explanatory Frameworks: Feminist Praxis across Generations."

Zillah Einsenstein

1. Zillah Eisenstein, *The Color of Gender: Reimagining Democracy* (Berkeley: University of California Press, 1994).
2. Zillah Eisenstein, *Capitalist Patriarchy and the Case for Socialist Feminism* (New York: Monthly Review Press, 1978).
3. On the Combahee River Collective, see chapter 1, note 1.
4. Bella Abzug (1920–1998) was a United States representative, lawyer, and antiwar activist. Bella cofounded the National Women's Political Caucus (NWPC) along with feminists Gloria Steinem, Shirley Chisholm, and Betty Freidan. She also cofounded the Women's Strike for Peace (WSP) with Dagmar Wilson in 1961. For her biography, see Bella Abzug, *Bella!: Ms. Abzug Goes to Washington*, ed. Mel Ziegler (New York: Saturday Review Press, 1972).
5. Zillah Eisenstein, *The Radical Future of Liberal Feminism* (New York: Longman Higher Education, 1981).
6. Valerie Jarrett served as senior adviser to President Barack Obama and assistant to the president for public engagement and intergovernmental affairs under the same administration.
7. At the time of this conversation, April 30, 2016, students across university and college campuses in India were protesting the institutional murder of Dalit scholar Rohith Vemula, caste discrimination, right-wing fundamentalism, and the growing suppression of independent critical thought on publicly funded university campuses, such as the University of Hyderabad in the south and Jawaharlal Nehru University in the north.
8. Narendra Modi, prime minister of India.
9. The Yazidis are a Kurdish religious minority who marry strictly within their religion.
10. See chapter 2, "Troubling Explanatory Frameworks: Feminist Praxis across Generations."
11. Nawal el Saadawi is an Egyptian feminist activist, educator, psychiatrist, and prolific writer. Tahrir Square is in Cairo, Egypt, where the Egyptian Revolution, 2011, began.

Toward a Politics of Refusal and Hope

1. See Sara Ahmed, *Willful Subjects* (Durham, NC: Duke University Press, 2014).
2. See Nicole Nguyen, A. Wendy Nastasi, Angie Mejia, Anya Stanger, Meredith Madden, and Chandra Talpade Mohanty, "Epistemic Friendships: Collective Knowledge-Making through Transnational Feminist Praxis," in

Dissident Friendships: Feminism, Imperialism, and Transnational Solidarity, ed. Elora Halim Chowdhury and Liz Philipose (Urbana: University of Illinois Press, 2016).

3. See The Movement for Black Lives, https://m4bl.net.
4. See Stand with Standing Rock, http://standwithstandingrock.net.
5. See Trans March, http://www.transmarch.org/about; Transgender Day of Remembrance, https://tdor.info/about-2; and Sylvia Rivera Law Project, https://srlp.org.
6. See BDS, https://bdsmovement.net/what-is-bds.
7. #Hokkolorob, #JusticeforRohith, #StandwithJNU, #breakthecurfew, #WhereIs Najeeb, and #PinjraTod: Break the Hostel Locks are just some of the campaigns that have been recently sparked by student activism in Kolkata, Hyderabad, New Delhi, Kerala, Punjab, and Uttar Pradesh.

Index

sexism, 39, 60, 68, 125, 146, 153,
172n12, 174n7
See also heteropatriarchy; misogyny;
patriarchy
Sexton, Anne, 57
sexuality, 6, 8, 28, 57, 62, 76–77, 96–97,
103, 105, 114, 163n1, 174n9
See also gay liberation movement;
heterosexuality; LGBTQ
movement; queerness
sexual violence, 14, 31, 42, 55, 63, 81,
108, 112, 117, 125–26, 141, 148
Sharecroppers Union, 73
Shaw University, 172n5
Sieder, Rachel, 112
Sierra, María Teresa, 112
Silvera, Makeda, 59–60, 170n18
Singh, Taveeshi, 10, 151–54
Sister Vision, 59, 170n18
Smith, Barbara, 141, 163n1
socialism, 17, 38, 53, 65, 68, 88, 95,
132, 170n31, 172n15
feminist, 17, 37, 86, 133–34, 169n8
social justice, 2–3, 6, 8–9, 12, 14,
49, 52, 54, 64, 68, 95, 109, 124,
129, 135, 154, 164n9, 165n16,
167n20, 170n21
social movements, 3
sociology, 63, 164n8, 176n12
Sosa, Mercedes, 58
South Africa, 3, 56, 100, 174n7
sovereignty, 6, 12, 49, 92, 172n15
Soviet Union, 65, 80
Spain, 79
Sri Lanka, 21, 164n6
Standing Rock Sioux, 12, 14, 49, 68,
129
state violence, 8, 56, 79, 86, 115
See also police violence; segregation
Steinem, Gloria, 177n4
Stewart, Helen, 17, 163n1

Sto:Loh nation, 170n19
structural adjustment policies (SAPs),
89–90, 173n5
See also neoliberalism
Stuckey, Johanna, 60, 169n24
Student Nonviolent Coordinating
Committee (SNCC), 73, 172n5
Suu Kyi, Aung San, 31
Swift brothers, 60
Switzerland, 26
Zurich, 21
Syracuse University, 78, 172n11
Syria
Aleppo, 148

Tanzania, 104
targeted regulation of abortion pro-
viders (TRAP) laws, 136
Temer, Michel, 126
Thatcher, Margaret, 89
THE General Body, 78
Third World Bookstore, 58
Third World liberation movement, 65
Third World Women's Alliance
Triple Jeopardy, 39
This Bridge Called My Back, 36, 166n8,
166n9
Tlatelolco massacre, 176n8
Tompkins, Mercedes, 163n1
transgender people, 16, 23, 43, 48, 96,
129, 148, 153, 167n18, 172n15
transnationalism, 3, 6–7, 15, 21, 23,
30, 90, 98, 126, 129, 148
Triple Jeopardy, 39
Trotsky, Leon
History of the Russian Revolution, 80
Trump, Donald, 6, 8, 32, 48, 67–68,
105, 127–29, 135, 141–42, 145,
147–48
See also "Muslim ban"
Turkey, 88